Praise for *Holy Adventure*

How often we shrink back from our Creator's larger purposes for our lives! Bruce Epperly challenges us to respond to the divine challenge, calling us to move out of our familiar patterns of living and experience the exhilaration of new adventure in companionship with our mighty God! This is the stirring book we need to rouse us from our apathy and boredom.

—LUCI SHAW
Author of *The Crime of Living Cautiously* and *Breath for the Bones*
Writer-in-residence, Regent College, Vancouver, BC

Through stories and scripture, Bruce Epperly suggests many ways readers can deepen and strengthen their relationship with God, who he suggests is constantly creative, evolving, and full of surprises. *Holy Adventure* is a testimony to the spiritual formation that occurs through ordinary living and daily practice.

—REV. JANE E. VENNARD
Senior Adjunct Faculty, Iliff School of Theology
Author of *A Praying Congregation: The Art of Teaching Spiritual Practice*

Through repeated practices of prayer and affirmation, Bruce Epperly invites us into the laboratory of spiritual transformation. Through holy imagination and adventurous action he invites us to move from being spectators on a tour to pilgrims on a world-transforming adventure. The holy adventure becomes an advent to a future of hope.

—KENT IRA GROFF
Retreat leader, spiritual guide, and author of
What Would I Believe If I Didn't Believe Anything? and *Writing Tides*

In the years since the horrific events of September 11, 2001, threw our nation into a spiritual tailspin, perhaps it was natural that a time of searching for easy answers and absolute truths would follow. *Holy Adventure* offers a way out of the immature cravings for certainty that have characterized our people in a time of fear. Epperly has developed a guide to spiritual practice for people who want to grow up, embrace mystery, and live from a place of love rather than fear.

—RICK UFFORD-CHASE
Executive Director, Presbyterian Peace Fellowship
Moderator, 216th General Assembly, Presbyterian Church (USA)
Stony Point Center, New York

HOLY
ADVENTURE

BRUCE G. EPPERLY

UPPER ROOM BOOKS®
NASHVILLE

HOLY ADVENTURE: 41 Days of Audacious Living
Copyright © 2008 by Bruce G. Epperly
All rights reserved.

Cover design: Left Coast Design, Portland, OR / www.leftcoast.com
Cover image: Getty / Iconica / Philip & Karen Smith
Interior design: Buckinghorse Design, Nashville, TN / www.buckinghorsedesign.com
First printing: 2008

Library of Congress Cataloging-in-Publication
Epperly, Bruce Gordon.
    Holy adventure : 41 days of audacious living / Bruce G. Epperly.
        p. cm.
    Includes bibliographic references.
    ISBN 978-0-8358-9970-3
    1. Spiritual life. 2. Christian life. I. Title.
    BV4501.3.E66 2008
    248.4—dc22

                                2008001784

Printed in the United States of America

CONTENTS

PART ONE

Life as a Holy Adventure

CHAPTER 1

Our Holy Adventure

hoose Your Own Adventure! When our son, Matt, was a child, we loved to read stories together. One particular series of children's books captured his attention and stimulated his imagination. "Choose your own adventure!" each book in the series proclaimed. Nearly every morning before school and then again at bedtime, the two of us embarked on adventures of imagination and companionship. The books challenged parent and child alike to make decisions that would shape the fictional journey ahead. Forced choices could lead to a dungeon or buried treasure, a storm at sea or a peaceful island. At each step of the way, the reader had to decide what the future would be for herself or himself. My son read these books with delight, for although various authors had initiated the stories, Matt's own decisions shaped the books' meaning for the present and the future. At an early age, my son learned that life was an adventure in which his moment-by-moment decisions would make a difference in his own and others' futures.

Choose Your Own Adventure! This is not just the title of a children's book series but also God's invitation to you and all creation. African-American mystic, teacher, and spiritual guide Howard Thurman described our lives as a holy adventure. In each moment we are confronted with choices, small and large, that will shape what we and the universe will become. Each moment reveals what the Celtic spiritual guides described as a "thin place" where persons can encounter the living God in ordinary time. While not usually as dramatic as the options in the Choose Your Own Adventure series, each choice we make in the course of the day awakens new possibilities for our relationship with God and the world we live in.

Just think of the adventure of Abraham and Sarah (Gen. 11–23). Comfortable and secure in old age, Abraham and Sarah experienced an unexpected call to adventure. They discovered that there was more to life than prosperity and predictability. A voice beckoned them toward new horizons, and no doubt they resisted its invitation until they realized that eventually they must make a choice. This divine voice, calling in dreams, synchronous encounters, restlessness, and dissatisfaction with everyday life, offered them a world of adventure with no safety net except its holy companionship in the wilderness. With fear and trembling, Abraham and Sarah risked everything on a venture into the unknown.

Whether or not you are aware of it, God calls you to an adventure in your time and place. When you pause to listen and take the first steps on God's adventurous path, everything changes! To see your life as a holy adventure that includes not only yourself but also your loved ones, the entire planet, and God, broadens the horizons of your life and influence on the world. Though the present moment and the immediate future are shaped by our previous decisions and a multitude of environmental factors, each choice we make can be the tipping point between health and illness, love and fear, and life and death in the unfolding adventure of a day or a lifetime. As spiritual children of Abraham and Sarah, we are called to listen and then say yes to the movements of God's holy adventure within the ordinary moments of our own lives.

Choose your own adventure! Our stories as contemporary followers of Jesus are part of a much larger narrative that embraces the insights of quantum physics, chaos theory, evolutionary biology, and holistic medicine. We share in the magnificent journey that joins cosmic adventure and human creativity. We are partners with God and one another in shaping the faith of the future and the health of the planet. While we may take pleasure in reading detective stories, classic tales of heroism, and biographies of great women and men, the fact is that our own lives and personal stories, despite their apparent anonymity and unimportance, can be as gripping as the fictional dramas that captivate our attention on a rainy afternoon or a long plane flight. Imagine reading these epic stories of literature in order to remind yourself of the wondrous possibilities of your own personal adventure. Imagine reading scripture for the same reason—to find inspiration and experience new possibilities as you face your own uncertain and exciting future!

There is nothing boring about any of our lives. Divine wisdom called each one of us into existence and invites us to choose our own adventures as the world unfolds in surprising ways each new day. Our everyday lives are part of a multibillion-year cosmic adventure that is still evolving in our ongoing partnerships with the Holy Adventure that we call God.

Like Abraham and Sarah, each of us has heard the Voice of adventure in the quiet moments and unexpected events of our own lives. God still speaks in our lives today. God invites you to be God's companion on a holy adventure!

FOR REFLECTION

Stop a moment right now and listen to the deeper rhythms of your life.

- What restlessness of spirit awakens you at night?
- What dreams in your life are still unfulfilled?
- What ideals can you reclaim that you have sacrificed for comfort or success?
- What seeds of new life lie dormant beneath the busyness of your everyday tasks?
- If you were to claim an adventure in companionship with God's holy adventure right now, where might it take you?
- What might happen in your life if you chose to affirm throughout the day the following words: "I am on a holy adventure with God as my companion"?

As they journeyed toward their own promised land, Abraham and Sarah discovered that what they imagined to be a solitary journey had global implications. Their choices would determine the future of a nation and a spiritual tradition that was still only a dream. Though currently child-less, they would give birth to a nation whose population would eventually be greater than the stars in the sky! So it is with our own adventures. Our choices radiate across the planet, tipping the balance between hope and despair, between life and death, in the lives of persons we'll never meet. Like Abraham and Sarah, we are blessed so we can be a blessing to others. Our adventure is not just about our own personal growth but also about healing the earth and the lives of everyone in it.

Take a moment to read Genesis 12:1-9. Notice that at each stopping point on the way to their promised land, Abraham and Sarah placed altars of gratitude to honor the Voice of Adventure. Perhaps they initially believed that these stone monuments would invoke the protection of the adventurous God. Later I suspect that Abraham and Sarah realized that the adventurous God did not need to be invoked by any human petition. God was always with them, surprising and guiding them throughout their journey.

Today their altars of gratitude and transformation remind us that the One who calls us to adventure also protects and guides us each step of the journey. Not bound by time or place or restricted to the faith of one people, God is our companion even in an unknown country. If we open to God's lively presence, we will discover that each place is consecrated and every encounter holy.

As we traverse our own spiritual frontiers, often with neither map nor compass, we need our own altars of transformation and hope to show us the importance of each day's journey, to awaken us to unexpected possibili-ties, and to inspire us to listen for God's voice of adventure in our everyday lives. These altars consecrate the most ordinary tasks as they awaken us to God's adventure in every moment of life.

In the pages ahead, we will create many altars of transformation and hope in partnership with God and one another through holy affirmations, quiet moments of renewal and retreat, imaginative prayers, prayerful com-panionship with fellow adventurers, and journeys of service and blessing. These altars of intentionality and awareness will serve as guideposts for our own holy adventure as companions and cocreators with the Holy Adventure who guides our steps each day.

For more than twenty years I have sought to share the vision of God's holy adventure in my roles as pastor, university chaplain, spiritual guide, healing companion, and seminary and university professor. My vision of God's holy adventure has been shaped not only by the contemporary and ancient wisdom of Christian theology and spiritual formation but also by my own encounters with God's holy adventure during times of challenge, conflict, and bereavement. I have found that the God who calls us to surprising and unexpected adventures gives us the courage and energy to be God's partners in transforming our lives and the world. The affirmations and meditations that I share in this book have changed my life and given me a vision of the future when I could find no path ahead. I have experienced and shared God's healing touch with others through these adventurous practices.

There is more! Legend has it that before the voyages of Columbus and other Western adventurers, European mapmakers inscribed the words *ne plus ultra*, "there is no more," at the far edges of their maps. After the voyages of Columbus and other European adventurers, these same mapmakers revised both their maps and their visions of reality. Although they had little knowledge of the wonders and dangers that lay beyond the far horizon, these mapmakers knew enough to inscribe the words *plus ultra*, "there is more," at the Western perimeters of their maps.

Thousands of years before these European travelers set foot on North America, Asian adventurers looked eastward, wondering if new lands lay beyond the horizon. They too expanded their vision of reality as they crossed the Bering Strait and traversed the North American wilderness, crying in amazement, "There is more!" as they pondered the adventures that lay ahead for them and their children.

The creed of all adventurers, from Abraham and Sarah to our own time—whether their journeys take place above the earth's atmosphere, in a laboratory, on an archeological dig, examining photographs from the Hubble telescope, exploring patterns of connectedness in the world of quantum physics, or walking the labyrinth—is always the affirmation "There is more!" What was mysterious becomes known, dreams become realities, and impossibilities become ordinary occurrences in our everyday lives. Then, after we rest awhile, the adventure beckons us forward toward new horizons and mysterious lands.

FOR REFLECTION

Think of your own life span. What "impossibilities" have you experienced and embodied in the course of your spiritual adventure?

- What personal "impossibilities" lie ahead of you?
- What new frontiers now beckon you professionally, relationally, and spiritually?
- Where do you imagine God's holy adventure guiding you in the days ahead?

As you venture toward new spiritual horizons, you will find good company in the Bible's own "choose your own adventure" stories! To Peter and his friends, worn-out and discouraged from an unsuccessful night's fishing, Jesus asked the impossible when he challenged them to "launch out into the deep and let down [their] nets for a catch" (Luke 5:4, NKJV). They knew that there were no more fish to be caught that day. But Jesus' deeper vision encompassed both the sea and their lives. He affirmed, "There is more!" Peter and his friends clearly had to revise their spiritual maps as they hauled an overwhelming catch into their boats.

Zacchaeus, the hated tax collector, imagined that the real world was no larger than his bank account until the day Jesus called him down from the tree. Small in stature and vision, Zacchaeus discovered that his life mission embraced the whole community and not just his own personal security, when he chose seeking justice, rather than accumulating wealth, as his life adventure from that day forth (Luke 19:1-10).

An invalid for nearly four decades, the man lying beside the pool must have thought that Jesus was insensitive or insane when the Galilean healer asked if he wanted to be healed and then commanded him to stand up and walk (John 5:1-9). But even after a lifetime as an invalid, he took a chance that there was more to his life than waiting passively for a healing. He could have collapsed both physically and spiritually, but he stood up—first in his imagination and then physically—as he picked up his bedroll and walked forward toward a new and challenging adventure. From now on he would be an initiator rather than a victim in the unfolding of his own holy adventure.

Mourning their brother's death, Mary and Martha discovered a new side to their grieving friend Jesus when he affirmed, "I am the resurrection and the life" and then commanded "Lazarus, come out!" (John 11:25, 43). Despite their grief and doubt, death was overcome, first in their imaginations and then in the celebrations of their dancing brother. There is more—to your life today and to God's holy adventure—than you can imagine!

When we choose to become partners in God's holy adventure, our world truly changes. New pathways and dimensions of life come out of nowhere. We discover that God doesn't have everything planned and that the story of our lives is open-ended. We discover that our adventure is part of a vastly larger spiritual adventure, for the universe itself is also open and unfinished. Yes, there are plotlines, shaped by our families of origin, genetics, culture, faith traditions, economic backgrounds, race and gender, and planetary history, but these do not tell the whole story. God is at work in our lives and has transformational visions for our futures, but these visions of the future are constantly shifting as we choose one path or another. Our choices partly shape God's next movements in the dance of life. God loves us too much to treat us like puppets who cannot shape our own destinies. Our input truly matters—to God and to the world—today and for generations to come! God's adventure is also open and unfinished, and God is constantly doing new things both to initiate and respond to our own creativity.

Yes, God has many visions of your possible futures and the futures of this planet. But God, like the authors of the Choose Your Own Adventure stories, has left many details and outcomes open for your creative input. God rejoices in our creativity and wants us to be willing partners in the creation of worlds to come. We can create scarcity, but we can also nurture abundant life on this good earth. There is more!

Living God's Holy Adventure

Adventurous faith joins a vision of God and the world in which we live; a promise that we can experience God; and practices for personal transformation, communion, and partnership with God. Healthy and sound visions of reality join our theological narratives, images, and metaphors of God with spiritual and ethical practices that transform our lives.

Author John M. Drescher tells the story of a dad's attempts to soothe his son's fears one night during a thunderstorm. The little boy called out, "Daddy, come. I'm scared."

"Oh, son," the father responded, in the hopes of reassuring his child. "God loves you; God will take care of you."

"I know God loves me and that God takes care of me," replied the boy. "But right now I want someone with skin on!"[1]

The heart of the Christian message is the affirmation that the God of adventure "has skin on." As John 1:14 says, "The Word became flesh and lived among us. . . . full of grace and truth." God's Word in Jesus dwells with us in flesh and blood, witnessing to the fact that although Jesus was one with God, Jesus was no exception to God's intimate relationship with the world. The God who touched Jesus' life also touches our own lives and every life. God is our ever-present companion, nearer to us than our next breath. Touching us and touched by us, God is constantly embracing and guiding us on our paths of adventure. Breathing through our lives, reviving us moment by moment, holding us when our resources seem depleted and all hope is gone—yes, God is always with us. Our God has skin!

In a world of adventure, our images of God must also be adventurous. A living God is open to novelty, change, and surprise. God doesn't need to control the future in order to be faithful to us today. A living God trusts creation enough to embrace a world in which even God does not fully know the outcome. A living God has the resources to adapt to every contingency we can imagine by nurturing new possibilities where we see only dead ends.

The adventurous God is wholly here and wholly now. This day and this place reveal God's fullness, for God is the Matrix of Life in whom "we live and move and have our being" (Acts 17:28). God is not caught in the web of God's own previous decisions. Rather, the living, growing, changing God gives life to all things, and in return, receives the gifts of all creation.

The poet of Psalm 139 felt God's nearness as he prayerfully considered his own holy adventure:

> Where can I go from your spirit?
> Or where can I flee from your presence? (v. 7)

When we imagine God as our constant companion, we experience God's presence not only in our rejoicing but also in our sorrow. Even when we run away from God or find ourselves overwhelmed by grief, depression, or hopelessness, we can experience God gently embracing and guiding us. God is with us, guiding our footsteps on a holy adventure, even when we feel most distant from God!

> If I ascend to heaven, you are there;
>   if I make my bed in Sheol, you are there.
> If I take the wings of the morning
>   and settle at the farthest limits of the sea,
> even there your hand shall lead me,
>   and your right hand shall hold me fast.
> If I say, "Surely the darkness shall cover me,
>   and the light around me become night,"
> even the darkness is not dark to you;
>   the night is as bright as the day,
>   for darkness is as light to you. (vv. 8-12)

All moments are God-filled and God-loved. All creatures are blessed by All-present God. Though a living God is uniquely and variably present in each moment of experience, God is fully present in all moments. Open to God's presence with all of his senses, the prophet Isaiah hears the angelic hymn of praise:

> Holy, holy, holy is the LORD of hosts;
> the whole earth is full of [God's] glory. (Isaiah 6:3)

Yes, the whole earth is full of God's glory, and that includes your own personal adventure as God's unique and beloved child! Isaiah's vision awakens us to God's creative presence in all things, including the ordinary moments of our own lives. We can sing praises to God as we worship in church or proclaim that "the heavens declare the glory of God" (Ps. 19:1, NIV) on a clear, starry night. But God's presence awakens us to that very same awe as we look at our own lives as unique and adventurous revelations of God. The twinkling stars, thousands of light-years away, declare the glory of God; but so do the gentle workings of a newborn baby's immune system, the nocturnal guidance each of us receives in dreams, the feel of a child's loving embrace, the emotions evoked by a familiar hymn in church, and the warmth of your beloved's kiss.

Divine creativity gives life to all things. Every moment of your life is guided by God's vision for your life and God's passion for your own expression of that vision. God shines in and through your unique creativity. The infinitely resourceful God responds to us just as we are. Jesus spoke of himself as a verdant vine and of his followers as abundant branches (John 15:1, 5-7). When we open to God's presence in our lives, divine energy flows effortlessly into our lives, and we flourish. When we ignore God's lively energy, our spirits wither, and we lose direction. This is not a threat but a reality of the spiritual adventure. God's vital energy is always streaming into our lives, but the shape and intensity of that flow is partly up to us! Our spiritual experiences and faith may make the difference between health and illness for ourselves and others. We may, by our own priorities, choose to open or close the door to the flow of God's life-transforming energy. Still, regardless of our current responses to God's dreams for our lives, God ceaselessly calls us to experience the fullness of life. God does not abandon any creature. God's love endures forever.

THE LISTENING GOD

God has skin, and God also has ears. God is a listening God who hears our lives in their entirety. Fully aware of life's complexity, God knows that each moment's decision arises out of an infinite constellation of prior moments and is shaped by our families of origin, economic backgrounds, education, ethnicity, gender, religious training, relationships, genetics, diet, and countless other factors. The listening God is our intimate companion, working in each moment of our lives to bring forth something of beauty. Like a poet or artist, God works with the materials God constantly receives from the world in order to help us become the poets and artists of our own lives.

The listening God has a vision for our lives and the universe that nurtures creativity and adventure in all things. In the immensity of the fifteen-billion-year cosmic adventure, God works gently, creating and re-creating, choosing one path and then taking another, pausing for a sabbath moment simply to experience the wonder of galaxies and quarks, dinosaurs and black holes. God has a vision for each moment as well as for the vast cosmic journey but trusts the universe enough to "let go" of the minute details of life in order to experience the process along with us. God rests so that we might also rest, knowing that we have a place in the fullness of God's love even if all of our purposes fail. The listening God is also the infinitely creative God whose love beckons us to new adventures and provides unexpected energy and options when our hope is nearly gone and our endurance ebbs.

CHAPTER 2

Holy Adventurers

While the spiritual adventure has many meanings, one significant aspect of spirituality is the ongoing discovery of our identity and vocation in the ever-flowing mirror of our experiences and encounters. This "choose your own adventure" book asks us to explore our images of who we are as humans in light of our images of God's companionship and creativity.

Our faith affirms that we are the children of an adventurous God who constantly calls us to choose our own adventures. God asks us to be partners in the planetary adventure. God will not undermine our moment-by-moment decision-making process. God does not want slaves and puppets but companions and cocreators. In the evolving dance of creation, the adventurous God also enjoys surprises that call on God to explore new possibilities for relationship and problem solving.

I would like to make six affirmations for your holy adventure as God's companion in healing the world. Part 2 builds on these theological and spiritual affirmations to chart *forty-one days of adventure* that will enrich your spiritual life. You will be able to experience God's adventure in your life and consciously choose to be God's partner in healing the world. I believe that the next forty-one days will provide a spiritual pathway to choosing God's own adventure in your unique and creative life.

1. *You are created in the image of God.* The biblical tradition envisages God as lively, creative, complex, and multifaceted. God is also seen

as loving, just, and innovative in response to the world. Created in God's image, we are challenged to embrace interdependence in ways that increase creativity, beauty, justice, and love. God seeks shalom—peace and wholeness—at every level of life, from cells to communities and nations. Our unique calling is to bring God's shalom to our relationships and the world.

2. *You are the light of the world.* As John's Gospel proclaims, "the true light, which enlightens everyone" has come into the world (1:9). Matthew's Gospel proclaims that "you are the light of the world" (5:14). You are a child of light, radiating God's wisdom and love. You are valuable as God's beloved daughter or son simply because you exist. Even when you go astray or turn your back on God's evolving dreams for your life and the world, God still loves you, gently inspiring you to find the adventure that best reflects your unique set of experiences and possibilities. You are God's shining light as you choose your own adventurous expression of divine wisdom. You are worthy of the love and abundant life God seeks for you.

3. *God inspires you in every moment.* God is a fountain of possibility and inspiration for every moment of your life. Often the adventure begins with an impossible dream that then takes on life in new behaviors and actions that transform your life and the world. When Jesus said, "Follow me" to Peter, James, and John, he invited them into a whole new realm of possibilities that each one could only realize in his own special way. This same inspiration is God's gift to you millisecond by millisecond.

4. *God is always with you.* Today, physicists describe for us an ever-expanding universe that has no absolute center. While this idea may be unsettling to those who see the cosmos as bounded and require that the earth be central and unique in God's plan for the universe, it is really good news for each one of us. As physicist John Jungerman notes, the universe is omnicentered, that is, "all points are equally the center."[1] This means that your life is always centered in the One True Center in whom "we live and move and have our

being" (Acts 17:28). You are never lost but have only forgotten where you are and who is both beside you and within you.

5. *Centered in God, your life truly matters.* The quest for meaning amid the vastness of the cosmos has always been a challenge to humankind. An ancient Hebrew pondered, "When I look at your heavens, . . . what are human beings that you are mindful of them?" (Ps. 8:3-4). But if God is omnipresent and omniscient, then you truly matter—not only to the ever-evolving universe and planet Earth but also to God's own dynamic journey. As infinitesimal as our lives may appear in a universe with billions of solar systems just like our own, God is a different God because of your life's contribution. As John Jungerman asserts, "If every point is the center in which the divine is immanent, then all aspects of the universe are equally important."[2]

While God chose Jesus of Nazareth to fully and uniquely reveal God's quest for wholeness, hospitality, and salvation, God also chooses you moment by moment to reflect and shape God's passion for beauty and wholeness in your time and place, in your family, in your workplace, and in your congregation.

6. *Our lives weave together the quest for wholeness for ourselves and for the universe.* Jewish mysticism affirms that our calling is to be God's partners in *tikkun 'olam*, or "mending the world." This is what it means to live out of your place in the body of Christ, in which, like the human body, health and illness radiate immediately and completely throughout the whole organism and can never be restricted to just one part of the divine matrix of love and light. Our joys and sorrows are joined with those of our planetary companions. We are artists of our experience, cocreators with God, and we are called to heal the world by the poetry of our lives.

CHAPTER 3

Purpose or Adventure?

You may have been reminded of another popular book while reflecting on the vision of God's open-ended, creative, and lively adventure and on your own role as a partner with God in healing the world. Many persons have found a greater sense of meaning through reading Rick Warren's *The Purpose Driven Life* or participating in Forty Days of Adventure groups. Warren charts a road map in which God chooses the most important events and encounters of our lives before we are born and without our input. Our personal calling, according to Warren's vision, is to discover and live out God's eternal purposes in our daily lives. We can find our true purpose only when we follow the directions and color inside the lines that God has already planned for us.

As you can see, I take a different pathway toward adventure. I believe God's holy adventure calls us to be creative and innovative right now as we listen for divine inspiration, and then to respond by coloring outside the lines and giving God something new as a result of our own personal artistry. In contrast to Rick Warren's view of God, I do not believe that God determines everything in advance but that we are invited to be God's companions in creating a future that is, to some degree, open and unfinished. I have coined the phrase "forty-one days of adventure" as a way of saying that neither God's work nor our own is complete and that God calls us to become creative companions in God's new and surprising creation. There is "something more" in the future for both God and our world.

God asks us to choose our own adventures. There is more to God and ourselves than we can imagine. As we explore the frontiers of our own experience, we will shape and transform the world to come. In this very moment we can make small decisions that will change the course of our lives and the lives of others. Look boldly toward the far horizon, for there is more! A holy adventure awaits you! Will you come and see?

A Prayer for the Adventure

This book is, from beginning to end, a prayer for guidance and inspiration. While I believe that God is constantly blessing us with new possibilities and the energy to achieve them, our prayers awaken us to God's movements in our lives and enable us to be God's partners in bringing beauty, justice, and wholeness to the world.

> Holy Adventure, like Abraham and Sarah, we don't fully know where the adventure will lead. But we do know that your love and inspiration never end. As we begin this journey of spiritual growth, inspire us to live by your adventurous vision. Awaken us to new ways of living out our faith. Give us courage when the way is uncertain. Give us open hearts so that we might bring beauty and love to those who journey beside us and to this good earth. In the name of our adventurous Christ, we pray. Amen.

PART TWO

Forty-One Days of Adventure

Introduction

As you become a conscious and willing partner in God's holy adventure, I need to point out that, whether or not you are aware of it, you are already on this holy adventure. Since your conception, God has been present in your life, encouraging you to dream, love, grow, and create. As you grew older, God was still present in your life, inviting you to grow in wisdom, stature, and service. You have felt this invitation in your heart and imagination as well as in synchronous encounters that have brought you to this time and to this book. In times of grief and transition, God has given you a vision of hope and abundant life. God has presented you with dreams and possibilities every step of the way, but God has left the details up to you. God needs artists and cocreators like you who embody God's creativity in your own unique way and add something to the world that God cannot do without your partnership.

Just as God is part of your life adventure, you are part of God's holy adventure. God calls you to claim the adventure that is yours in order to bring wholeness and beauty to the world. But when the going isn't easy and we get discouraged, we can take heart in the promise that God's adventure lives through us even when we are unaware of it. When we say yes to God's adventure by practices of self-awareness and committed actions, we become conscious partners with God in transforming the world. By saying yes, we open the door to the One who is always knocking, and we yield to God's ever-flowing streams of creative energy and lively possibility.

As I look at God's presence in the world, I visualize our lives in terms of creativity and surprise. I believe that God is constantly present in our lives, giving us dreams and possibilities and the energy to bring them to birth in the world. These dreams and possibilities are not conjured up in some abstract eternity; they are emerging in "real time" in the context of our environment, families, and lives today. God gives us a dream and invites us to improvise. God likes creativity, artistry, and adventure. The living God is not stuck in a preplanned vision of the universe. God does not determine the unchanging future in eternity but lives toward the future in terms of the constantly creative present moment. God is constantly creating, and so are we!

These forty-one days of adventure point to the evolving and open-ended nature of our lives as God's beloved children. God wants us to be imaginative cocreators in the ongoing evolution of the universe. Our purposes emerge in the concrete details of our relationships with God and our planetary companions, not in a scripted enactment.

In the weeks ahead, I invite you to "choose your own adventure" as an intentional participant in God's holy adventure. Each "day"—and a day can mean twenty-four hours or two weeks—weaves together a vision, promise, and practices. I will share a vision of God and our calling in the world as it relates to a specific aspect of the human adventure and invite you to experience that vision in your personal life through spiritual practices such as:

1. *theological reflections* to enable you to experience an adventurous world in which your choices make a difference both to God and your neighbors
2. *prayers for the adventure* to inspire you to see your life as an adventure in companionship with God
3. *spiritual affirmations* to transform your mind and awaken you to undreamed-of possibilities for yourself and the world
4. *imaginative prayers* to expand your consciousness and deepen your faith in God's presence in your life and your vocation as God's partner in healing the world
5. *adventurous actions* to embody your spiritual growth in the transformation of everyday life through your positive relationships with

family and friends, the life of your congregation, and your role as God's partner in healing the world

A Process Note

Each spiritual practice provides a way to experience personally and directly God's adventure in your life and to live out a lively and holistic Christian vision of reality. Each day is related to all the others, emerging from, reflecting, and supporting the insights of all the other days, in terms of this Christian vision of reality as it relates to our understanding of God, Christ, our vocations in the human and cosmic adventures, healing and wholeness, and the realities of death and everlasting life. Accordingly, the theological insights and spiritual exercises often overlap as they explore the multifaceted and interdependent nature of God's presence in our lives and vocations as God's companions in living, creating, and dying.

A rabbi once raised a question about the burning bush that inspired Moses to leave his flock and become a national leader: "Why did the bush burn but never get consumed by the fire?" His colleague responded, "It burned without being consumed so that one day, as Moses passed by the burning bush, he would finally notice it!"

The spiritual exercises enable us to live the theological visions we affirm. They enable us to see the many "burning bushes" God has placed along our pathway. Because these exercises are meant to inspire your unique vocation in God's holy adventure, feel free to adapt them to your own particular life situation and experience of God. Don't hesitate to skip exercises that do not speak to your current spiritual journey. See the exercises as invitations to experience your own spiritual adventure more deeply rather than as assignments to complete. The goal of the exercises is to invite you to embrace your own unique and holy adventure in your own time and place, and with your own gifts and life experiences.

The practices, or exercises, are intended to address different personality types, religious experiences, worship styles, and ways of encountering the world. While I encourage you to attempt all three practices—affirmations, imaginative prayer, and adventurous action and service—in the course of this study, some practices will more directly address your spiritual needs, depending on whether your primary life orientation is intellectual, imaginative, or active. Take time to playfully explore new ways of experiencing God's multifaceted presence in your life. You can't fail—for the path you take is always holy, and you are always in God's care!

Our lives evolve moment by moment at no particular speed. Growth can occur when we least expect it, sometimes through pregnant waiting, other times through decisive action. As you live through each day, move at your own spiritual cadence. Do not feel that you must complete every exercise. Spiritual growth is not about inflexible goal seeking or unalterable purposes but about living at the tempo that best reflects your embodiment of God's dream for you and your world. Your life has countless purposes, and these purposes constantly evolve as you experience new things. Please rest assured that you don't have to achieve anything spiritually in order to be loved, nor will God forsake you if you fail in achieving your moment-by-moment calling. While God's eternal love calls us to take our adventures seriously, remember that God's holy adventure is everlasting and evolving in and through us. God is our holy companion! Choose your own adventure as God's partner in spiritual growth and global healing. Divine possibilities await you at every turn!

"This is the day that the LORD has made; let us rejoice and be glad in it" (Ps. 118:24). Go forth in peace and wonder, for God is with you on your holy adventure.

TRANSFORMING GOD

The apostle Paul asserted, "Do not be conformed to this world, but be transformed by the renewing of your minds" (Rom. 12:2). At the heart of the spiritual adventure you are now beginning is the recognition that our images of God shape our behavior, values, self-image, ethical commitments, and the quality of God's presence in our lives and in the world. Our life-transforming images of God reflect the dynamic interplay of the living God, scripture, our communities of faith, our own experience, and the evolving cultural and planetary history. To claim our conscious experience as part of this lively matrix is to recognize that everything is in perpetual motion. While this constant transformation can be spiritually and theologically unsettling, it is also the foundation for hope and creativity. In a changing universe, we have the power to change ourselves and our images of God so that they can become more like the living God, whose love is revealed in Jesus of Nazareth and in every moment of our own lives.

As we begin our journey, I caution all adventurers to remember that we must always speak of God with great humility. The beginning of wisdom is, as scripture proclaims, awe and reverence of God. In this regard, it is helpful to remember that Christians have historically held two profound spiritual truths in creative tension:

1. *No word, image, or description of God is completely accurate.* As the Zen Buddhist proverb affirms, "Do not confuse the moon with the finger that points at it." Our constant recognition that all God-images are incomplete and imperfect is our greatest protection against inflexible and authoritarian images of God. God cannot be contained by our images and metaphors, scripture, church, ideology, reason, science, or even our own personal experiences. God is always more than we can imagine!

2. *God is revealed in all things, including our images, metaphors, scriptures, and experiences.* God does not hide from us. The God of scripture, tradition, and spiritual experience wants to be known. Always present in our experience, God can be found everywhere and in anyone. Right this minute, God is addressing you through the words on this page, my positive intention in writing them, and your response to them. God is also speaking to you through your dreams, insights, relationships, and creativity. God calls to you through the insights of medical researchers, physicists, biologists, and paleontologists whose discoveries shape our understanding of ourselves and the universe.

As Christians, we are invited to be *playful mystics*. We can delight in God's handiwork in all things. We can embrace God as we hug our spouse or partner, play Scrabble with a child, or celebrate our successes. We can breathe the living God in every moment's respiration.

For Reflection

What would it mean for you to see all places as holy ground and all persons around you as holy persons?

Play with your images of God, drawing the outlines of God's nature as you might a beautiful landscape, and know that God is always more beautiful and complex than our best artistry and that our deepest insights capture only the smallest fragment of God's wholeness. There is more!

We are called to let our most inspirational images of the Holy One guide our paths. As with all adventurers, we seek to construct the most accurate maps of God's nature, knowing that reality is always more than the maps we make. These maps help us experience God's life in our lives. They shape our tools for personal transformation and the practices that awaken us to God in our lives. They help us create altars of gratitude and faithfulness. Encountering God in the intimacy of our experience, we shape our own holy adventures and support the holy adventures of our earthly companions.

Through the seven days of exercises in this chapter, we will explore our images of the living God through affirmations, imaginative spiritual practices, and healing actions, grounded in the evolving wisdom of scripture and theological reflection. As you make your holy affirmations about God, I invite you to recognize that adventurers in other faiths and other branches of Christianity may have experienced unique aspects of the Holy One. Our own images of God and the human adventure are tested and grow in conversation with alternative visions of the Ultimate Reality. Still, as a point of spiritual departure for our forty-one-day pilgrimage, I invite you to affirm the following images of the Holy Adventure that inspire our own personal and planetary adventures.

- God is alive and moving through all creation.
- God is at work in our lives, in culture and politics, in science, and in the evolving planetary adventure.
- Divine creativity is universal and ongoing.
- God's love embraces all reality, including nonhuman life.
- God seeks justice and wholeness for all things, and works through our imperfection and the imperfection of our families, communities, and institutions to bring forth a world of beauty and wonder.
- God is doing a new thing and revealing new truths. God still speaks.

To awaken to the truth of these affirmations is to embrace God's perpetual transformation even in difficult times. God has dreams for your life that lie beyond any that you can imagine. Still, God has left the details to your own creativity. Don't let past experiences—even your previous positive or negative images of God—limit you as you open to this transformative power. Let the adventurous God invite you to experience God and the world in new and surprising ways.

DAY 1

God Loves the Whole World, No Exceptions

For God so loved the world that God gave us the Christ.
—John 3:16, AP

I n the Christian tradition, every spiritual adventure begins with the question of the size or stature of the God we worship. *How big is your God? Is God big enough to guide the fifteen-billion-year cosmic adventure, encompassing billions of galaxies like our own Milky Way?[1] Is God big enough to embrace the complexities of your life? Is God big enough to embrace the stranger and the enemy?*

The quest for stature in understanding God's relationships with foreigners and strangers lay at the heart of Hebraic and Christian journeys. Was God a tribal deity, whose love extended only as far as the chosen people, or did God's concern embrace the whole cosmos, including the enemy and the nonhuman world? The current culture and religious wars that characterize the American political landscape, the Holy Land, and Southwest Asia remind us that these theological questions are still a matter of life and death.

Today many images of God lack sufficient stature to embrace the pluralism and complexity of our time. I recall once hearing an evangelist describing how to get to heaven. He proclaimed that if you boarded a spaceship, left our solar system, and headed beyond the Milky Way, you would eventually arrive at a place called heaven. He was equally clear that the only way you could board that spaceship was by believing every word in the Bible and having a datable conversion experience. Tribal, earth-centered faiths abound in our world today. These faiths demand absolute doctrinal certainty and image a divine sovereign who separates the world in terms of friend and foe, saved and unsaved, and asks followers to do likewise!

In contrast, an adventurous God embraces the whole universe, and so can we. As John's Gospel affirms, "For God so loved the world that he gave his only Son" (3:16). More than a placard to be raised at a sports event, this passage affirms that the mission of Jesus was directed to the whole earth, not just to a particular people or faith tradition. Jesus proclaimed that God's sun shines on the righteous and the unrighteous alike (Matt. 5:45). Those who had been excluded from religious observances found themselves embraced by God's loving arms and welcomed at God's banquet table. Whoever we are and wherever we go in the course of our adventures, we are always in God's loving hands.

Listen again to those words of scripture: "For God so loved the world." God's love is not limited to humankind. All creation bears the divine image and reflects God's love. When I was five, my brother and I spent a few days with our parents' friends in Morro Bay, California. Hour after hour, I played with their dog, Taffy. Being a pious child, I asked the dog's owner, Mrs. Brown, "Will Taffy go to heaven?" Her response shocked me. "Of course not," she replied. "Jesus died to save us from our sins, not to save dumb animals!" At that moment, I knew that the God I had been hearing about in church was either too small or too petty to be worshiped. Even as a child, I knew in my heart that whatever we love shares in God's eternity.

The adventurous God loves fox terriers, Siamese cats, and the color purple! God has sufficient stature to reach out to Islamic fundamentalists and American entrepreneurs alike, as well as Pentecostal preachers and progressive professors. This same God who loves the entire world in all its colorful diversity also loves you in a special way. You are God's beloved child, and so is everyone else.

A Prayer for the Adventure

Loving and creative God, we thank you that you have called us to be lovers and creators like you. Give us the vision and the energy to love as you love, embracing the lost and lonely, and the vulnerable and antagonistic. Help us to experience your unexpected presence in the cry of a child in Darfur, an Islamic mullah, a neighbor dying of cancer, a goose flying homeward, and the lightning bugs of a summer evening. Let us go forth on this adventure with your blessing, blessing all of creation in love and care. Amen.

CHOOSING YOUR OWN AFFIRMATION

Physicians speak of the placebo effect, in which positive beliefs are translated into good physical health. We live by our deeply held affirmations. What we believe deep down shapes the cells of our bodies and guides our day-to-day behavior. Affirmations, or positive theological statements about ourselves and the world, change the way we experience life, first consciously and then unconsciously. What we affirm becomes the lens through which we experience the universe one moment at a time. An adventurous God invites us to imagine a lively world in which divine possibilities lure us toward new personal and community adventures. Our affirmations are concretely proclaimed and lived out in our day-to-day lives. They enable us to see holiness where others see the mundane. Meditate a few moments on a poem by Elizabeth Barrett Browning as an inspiration to your own spiritual practices.

> Earth's crammed with heaven,
> And every common bush afire with God;
> But only he who sees, takes off his shoes,
> The rest sit round it and pluck blackberries.[2]

Try these affirmations, or create your own personal affirmations as a means of transforming your images of God on your own holy adventure. A good way to practice spiritual affirmations is to repeat them several times during the course of the day, especially in challenging situations. Whenever you feel as if you are losing your spiritual bearings, return to these holy affirmations. You may also choose to write them on note cards to look at during the day. Though at first they may seem counterfactual, these spiritual affirmations reflect the deeper realities of our life and faith. They will remind you that there is always "more" to God's presence in your life than you can imagine. In living with these affirmations, you will grow in companionship with the infinitely growing God.

- God loves the world—no exceptions.
- God loves me.
- God loves me, (*fill in your name*), yesterday, today, and tomorrow.
- God loves (*fill in the name of a family member or friend*).
- God's love embraces both _____ and _____ (*name two political, military, or personal adversaries*).

YOUR HOLY IMAGINATION

Images are as powerful as words in transforming, first, our experience of the world, and then, the world itself through our thoughts and actions. Our faith lives by images, and images invite us to sense new dimensions of the Holy Adventure in which we live.

Whenever I speak to an unfamiliar audience, I take a moment to imagine myself speaking meaningful and life-changing words to attentive friends. Often I choose one person to be my "angel" or "messenger of God" in the group. I make it a point to pray for that person and affirm that my words will contribute to her or his spiritual growth. Occasionally, I introduce myself to this person before the program. That way, I am always at home, even in unfamiliar settings.

In this spiritual exercise, simply relax a moment, paying attention to your breath as it flows into your belly and then gently out again. Feel the joy of being alive at this time and place. Experience each breath as embodying God's creative and enlivening presence in your life. Then, with each breath, focus on a person in your life—either an intimate friend or relative, a coworker, or someone in the news about whom you have a special concern. Experience each breath as God's holy presence in this individual's life. With each breath, feel the deep connection that you share with the other, whether that person is a beloved companion or a hated international figure or group.

In my prayer life, I surround my wife, son, colleagues, good friends, and even difficult and challenging people in God's light and love in order to affirm our common identity as God's beloved children. As I image their well-being, I too am transformed and become whole.

LIVING ADVENTUROUSLY

Thomas Merton described the spiritual life as "contemplation in a world of action." Our task is to notice, pause, affirm, imagine, and then act on our awareness of God's presence in our lives and then extend God's presence toward others in our ordinary and extraordinary encounters.[3] We are to be theologians of the hand and heart as well as of the mind! As we live our adventures, we will discover that all places are holy and all encounters healing.

Mother Teresa once spoke of seeing God in all of God's disguises. She believed that "every person is Christ for me . . . I see God in every human being."[4] Today's practice involves simply going through your day with the awareness that God is present in every person and encounter. In the Hindu tradition, people often greet one another with the word *namaste*, meaning "The spirit in me greets the spirit in you." In this frame of mind, throughout the day, look more deeply at the persons you encounter. You might even say to yourself, "The Christ in me greets the Christ in you" with every encounter and ring of the phone. See beyond others' behavior and appearance. See their essential holiness. See them as God's beloved children, sons, daughters, and animal companions. As you begin to speak to others, let this new perspective guide your words and behavior. Let your words and acts address God's holy adventure working in their lives as well as your own.

For example, take a moment as you shop today to see the clerk as God's beloved child. Notice what is unique about the clerk as a person. Though you may be waiting in a long line, you will begin to experience a sense of holiness instead of impatience and anger. Or, instead of succumbing to your own version of "road rage," see the divine light and love present in the one who just honked at you or cut you off on the highway. Say a quick prayer for that person's well-being and safety on the road to his or her destination. You will discover that your own rage metamorphoses into a feeling of peace and wholeness. As simple as these behavioral changes may be, they will transform your life and, quite possibly, your lived experience of God.

DAY 2

God Is Our Companion
in Every Situation

Nothing in all creation can separate us from God's love for us in Christ Jesus our Lord!

—Romans 8:39, CEV

What is your greatest fear? What situation sends shivers down your spine whenever you think about it? Take a moment to let the images and feeling emerge.

Adventurous living is not for the fainthearted. There are few safety nets for those who explore the frontiers beyond their maps of reality. But the One who calls us to venture beyond our known world is our companion every step of the way. The One who inspires also guides; the One who challenges also reaches out to catch us when we fall. We can still fail to achieve our goals, but no failure is final when God is our companion. God's light and love conquer all things, even death.

The apostle Paul was a spiritual risk taker who knew what it meant to trust God with his life. Beaten, imprisoned, persecuted, and no doubt frightened at the prospect of his death as well as the reality of his own inner struggles, Paul depended on God to be his companion as he ventured into unfamiliar and dangerous territory in order to share the good news of God's love. Looking back on his adventures, Paul proclaimed:

> For I am convinced that neither death, nor life, nor angels, nor rulers, nor things present, nor things to come, nor powers, nor height, nor depth, nor anything else in all creation, will be able to separate us from the love of God in Christ Jesus our Lord. (Rom. 8:38-39)

Today, nothing can separate you from the love of God, not even your greatest fears.

In one of his sermons, Martin Luther King Jr. told of discovering God in the midst of the darkest night of the spirit. During the first days of the Montgomery, Alabama, bus boycott, King received an anonymous, life-threatening phone call. Trembling with fear and unable to sleep, King went downstairs to make a cup of coffee. As the coffee perked, he poured out his soul to God: "I am here taking a stand for what I believe is right. But now I am afraid. The people are looking to me for leadership, and if I stand before them without strength and courage, they too will falter. I am at the end of my powers. I have nothing left. I've come to the point where I can't face it alone." In that moment, King felt a quiet presence that would forever change his life. An inner voice whispered, "Stand up for righteousness, stand up for truth. God will be at your side forever." Although there was no promise that he would escape trouble, King recalled, "My uncertainty disappeared. I was ready to face anything. The outer situation remained the same, but God had given me inner calm."[5]

Inner calm in the face of suffering, tragedy, and threat comes from trusting that God is with us no matter what befalls us. In life and in death, we are in God's eternal care. Though God will not overturn the laws of nature to protect us, God will enable us to find a way where there seems to be no way. With God as our companion, we can experience deep calm amid the storm.

God's love is constant and intimate. God knows your deepest fears and greatest hopes. God experiences your struggle to do something new and creative and to change old, harmful behaviors. Whether you initially succeed or fail, God will not abandon you but will guide and open up new possibilities to you each step of the way.

A Prayer for the Adventure

Amid the storm, you are with us, O God. Help us to sense your calm presence when our hearts are anxious and afraid. Help us to experience your strength giving us strength and your power giving us courage in the quest for justice and healing. Amen.

CHOOSING YOUR OWN AFFIRMATION

Affirmations are both preventative and responsive in nature. In your quest to deepen your spiritual life, take time to live with positive spiritual affirmations when life is pleasant and easy. At such times, they will build up your spiritual strength and shape your vision of reality in ways that will sustain you when things are not so pleasant or easy. Remember the truth of these same affirmations when life's challenges confront you and you are at your personal limits. They will remind you of the reality of God's faithfulness sustaining and strengthening you in the midst of conflict, pain, and tragedy. Take time to repeat the following affirmations, or other affirmations of your choice, throughout the day.

- Nothing can separate me from the love of God.
- (*Name a particular fear*) cannot separate me from the love of God.
- God is my companion in every situation.
- God is my companion in (*name a particular situation*).

YOUR HOLY IMAGINATION

Take a moment simply to be still, breathing slowly and gently. With every breath, experience God's loving energy entering your life. Once you have reached a state of calm, take a moment to imagine some person or event that frightens you. Spend some time examining that fear—see it, feel it, and reflect on its impact on your life. Notice your breathing as you experience your fear. Where has fear limited you? What would it be like to face this threat without fear?

As you imagine the fear, feel the presence of God in that situation, perhaps in terms of your breath, a holy light, or loving arms embracing you. Whenever you feel afraid, take time for a deep breath and imagine God as your companion. As your experience of God heightens, see the object of your fears receding in importance and power. (While fear is not to be denied, our relationship with God places our fears in a new context. They cannot ultimately defeat us, because God is with us, in us, and around us, giving us the insights and resources we need to respond creatively to life's threats.) Feel God completely with you, and let God's promise and presence echo in your whole being, "Nothing can separate you from my love."

LIVING ADVENTUROUSLY

Whether or not we are aware of it, we constantly shape and interpret our experiences, in addition to being shaped and interpreted by them. Despite the impact of past events that were out of our control or that brought out the worst in us, we are artists of each moment of our lives in every new moment. This is good news! With God as our companion, transformation is possible in every situation.

For years I avoided any form of artwork. My childhood insecurities about drawing and painting dominated my adult life. Only under duress would I attempt to draw something as simple as a stick figure until one of my friends threw herself a fiftieth birthday party, at which she invited her guests to do watercolors. As the other guests began to paint, I was forced to make a decision—to paint or not to paint. With all my insecurities, I began to paint, and I had fun! While none of my work will ever be hung at the Smithsonian or the Museum of Modern Art, I discovered that I could paint and enjoy it. I discovered that I didn't even have to be good in order to be an artist.

> Despite the impact of past events that were out of our control or that brought out the worst in us, we are artists of each moment of our lives in every new moment. This is good news!

You are the artist of your experience. Take a moment and ponder something you have avoided doing because of fear of failure or looking silly. If the activity is one that is essentially safe for you to perform, take a chance. Paint a picture; go horseback riding; lead a discussion group; tutor in the inner city. Every journey begins with the first step, however small. Take the first step on your holy adventure today!

DAY 3

God Is Still Creating

I am about to do a new thing;
now it springs forth, do you not perceive it?

—Isaiah 43:19

ot far from my home in Lancaster, Pennsylvania, a controversy raged about whether or not "intelligent design" could be taught in public schools as an alternative to the theory of evolution. The proponents of intelligent design saw evolution and divine creativity as mutually exclusive. In their eyes, the phrase "theistic evolution" was an oxymoron. To them, God created the earth in six twenty-four-hour days and then rested from any further creativity. Despite the biblical witness that God is alive and creative in human and nonhuman history, they could not imagine divine creativity at work in bringing forth new species or doing new things within the nonhuman world.

While an adventurous spirituality does not claim to provide scientific data that proves God's ever-transforming power throughout the universe, the vision of God's holy adventure boldly asserts that God is continually working in our personal, planetary, and cosmic evolution, and reminds us that we live in the "eighth day" of creation. Though scripture speaks of God resting on the sabbath, this divine rest is symbolic of God's gift of freedom and creativity to the whole world. God's sabbath invites us to become God's conscious partners in shaping the future of the planet and our own communities. God's sabbath rest also reminds us that we can also take time for rest and play, trusting that divine creativity provides for our deepest personal and planetary needs.

I believe that God is still creating. New possibilities are always emerging in our lives and in the planetary adventure. Though we live in a risky universe in which happy endings cannot be presumed, we can choose to become God's partners in an open system whose best days lie in the future.

In speaking of the all-creating wisdom of God, John's Gospel proclaims that "all things came into being through [Divine Wisdom], and without [Divine Wisdom] not one thing came into being. . . . The true light, which enlightens everyone, was coming into the world" (1:3, 9, AP). All things are enlightened by God's constantly creating wisdom. The true light is coming into the world today, and God is doing a new thing in the universe and in your own life and mine!

A Prayer for the Adventure

Holy Wisdom, creating all things in light, growing all things in darkness, encompass us with your creative power. Speak within our bodies, minds, and spirits. Enlighten and enliven our hearts. Let the glow of your holy light flow through us, bringing wholeness and enlightenment to others. Let your divine creativity inspire us to the creation of a new and just humanity, whose works bring life and love to this good earth. Amen.

CHOOSING YOUR OWN AFFIRMATION

If we actively respond to God's invitation to be God's partners in healing the universe, we will discover that God continually proposes new possibilities for us to embody and then responds to what we have done. Like a good parent, God rejoices at our creativity and delights in our inventiveness. Throughout the day, I invite you to join God in claiming your unique creative adventure by repeating and reflecting on the following spiritual affirmations.

- God is constantly creating the universe and my life.
- God and I are partners in God's new creation.
- Divine creativity is revealed in (*some aspect of my life*).
- Divine creativity is revealed in (*a particular life situation*).

Your Holy Imagination

Spiritual guide Frederick Buechner invites us to listen to our lives. According to Buechner, God calls you to "listen to your life. See it for the fathomless mystery that it is."[6] Our lives are a holy adventure in which each moment provides new possibilities for Spirit-filled living. Take a moment to relax, breathing in God's calm presence. In this quiet moment, remember the moments when your life most reflected God's creativity. Experience the joy of being fully alive. Rejoice in those memories. Take some time to journal about these spiritual high points if you wish. Give thanks for God's creative presence in your life.

Listen to your life today. Where do you see new possibilities emerging? What dreams inspire you as you look toward tomorrow? Visualize yourself embodying these dreams in your daily life. Take time to experience God as your constant and loving companion in bringing these dreams to birth. Rejoice and give thanks for your creative future in partnership with God.

Living Adventurously

Inspired by God's vision of shalom, the wholeness of all things, Jewish mystics saw the vocation of humankind as *tikkun 'olam*, or "mending the world." We are God's partners in healing the planet. The Genesis story of the primordial garden reminds us that the earth can become a place of beauty, wonder, and shalom. A healed earth joins the primordial beginnings of life and the innocence of nature with the complexity and beauty of human creativity.

As you listen to your life in light of your spiritual high points, commit yourself to becoming God's partner in "mending the world." Look at your own unique sphere of action. Just for today, what *one* act can you do to bring healing to the earth?

Perhaps you may concretely choose to pick up litter at a park or nature trail. You may call your representatives to register your opinion about an ecological issue, the care of vulnerable persons, universal health insurance, or the expansion of human rights to include persons marginalized as a result of birthplace or sexual orientation. You may challenge national priorities that value military might over personal well-being.

The world is saved one moment at a time and one person at a time.

Your action can be the decisive "tipping point" between life and death for yourself and the planet.

DAY 4

We Are All Part of God's Holy Adventure

Who knows? Perhaps you have come . . . for just such a time as this.
—Esther 4:14

The whole universe, from an infant's smile to the Milky Way, reflects the subtle and constant creativity of God. God gives us space to create, even as God creates within us and alongside us. John Calvin once spoke of the world as the theater of God's glory. Divine glory—the flowing forth of God's creative love to bring beauty to life—is both serious and playful business. In every moment, God seeks in a unique and personal way to bring forth beauty, wonder, and wholeness out of the many factors that constitute your experience and the ongoing planetary adventure.

Your life has a place in God's vision of the universe. Your life is not determined fully by God or anyone else, but neither is it random or accidental. Within each moment of your life is a dream that arises from the interplay of many factors, including your previous decisions, family of origin, environment, and culture. Within each of these influences, God is at work to give you a vision of what this moment can most fully be. God has many dreams for your life, and each dream is lived out one moment at a time.

Traditional religious language speaks of discovering your "vocation" or "calling" as a primary goal of life. Your vocation is not only about your own self-actualization but also about your contribution to the universe, the planet, and your family. It is about living God's dream in your own wonderfully unique way.

While I do not believe that God has planned our lives from eternity, I do affirm that God works in every moment to inspire our own creativity as a means of bringing joy and beauty to ourselves and to the universe. Your life is your gift to God, and your gifts arise from the intricate interplay of your passions, talents, dreams, and experiences with the world's needs.

Our lives are not fully determined by God, our genes, family of origin, environment, or any other single factor, but they emerge from a world of multiple synchronous relationships. Every moment is the right moment for personal transformation. In every moment, God weaves together persons and possibilities in order to create a world of meaning and beauty.

The spiritual adventure is a process of noticing God's many revelations within every encounter of life. Like Jacob, we are called to pause and reflect on the angelic presence in even the most desolate spots. Like Moses, we are challenged to stop before the constantly burning bush that we fail to notice in our purpose-driven days.

The Hebraic tradition celebrates Esther for her role in saving her people. A member of the king's court, Esther kept a low profile until she was called to be the "first lady" of the empire. When she heard of the plot to destroy her people, she initially kept quiet, masking her own ethnicity. Then she sprang into action and saved her people when her spiritual guide, Mordecai, challenged her with the insight that God had brought her to this place of power "for just such a time as this" (Esther 4:14). Esther is remembered today because she paused long enough to listen for God's voice in Mordecai's mentoring and then had the courage to take a chance that the God who inspired her would also guide and protect her.

In synchronous moments of divine wisdom, human choice, and creativity, your life is unfolding "for just such a time as this." In each moment, you are given many good options to shape your life and the planet. Pause for a moment. Listen to your life. Can you experience the dream God has for you and the unique creativity that you bring to this moment?

A Prayer for the Adventure

For just such a time as this, O Holy Adventure, give us vision and the courage to live your dream for our lives. Let us be bold in aspiration and adventurous in action. Let us speak for justice and act for healing for just such a time as this. In the name of Jesus Christ the Healer. Amen.

CHOOSING YOUR OWN AFFIRMATION

Awakening to divine wisdom and synchronicity is a matter of mindfulness and self-awareness. It is also a matter of choosing to be open and then acting on the inspirations you receive. Today's affirmations are a theological searchlight that can enable you to become more aware of the intersections of your deepest wisdom and God's dream for you in each moment and encounter. As you repeat these affirmations or ones that you have chosen, trust that God is guiding you for just such a time as this!

- Divine wisdom is at work in my life right now.
- Divine creativity is at work in my life right now.
- I experience divine guidance in (*a particular situation*).
- I awaken to divine inspiration in synchronous moments and encounters.

YOUR HOLY IMAGINATION

Once again as you prepare to let your imagination join God's imagination for your life and the world, take time to be still, knowing that God is working within the world and your life circumstances, whatever they may be. Visualize yourself sitting in your favorite place of beauty. Experience the unique beauty and wonder of this place. Feel its peace and tranquillity. In that peaceful moment, look at your life today, pondering the many relationships and responsibilities of your life at this time. What relationships and responsibilities call you forward into newness this day?

In the course of your reflections, notice that you are not alone. Jesus the teacher and spiritual guide is with you. What would you like to share with Jesus? How does he respond? During your conversation, Jesus invites you to reflect on your calling. What images come to mind? How do you respond to his question? As you finish sharing, Jesus reminds you, "I will be with you to guide and inspire you as you live out your unique expression of God's dream. You are not alone." Take a moment to give thanks for God's constant creativity and inspiration in your life and in the world.

You may choose to journal about your experience or simply remind yourself throughout the day of God's constantly inspiring presence and your calling to respond in your own unique way.

Living Adventurously

Be attentive today to synchronous moments that characterize your life. Holy synchronicity joins God's dream and our deepest wisdom with the dynamic flow of life. We are connected with everyone and everything in the grand ecology of the universe. Awaken to the divine synchronicity that is present in your everyday life. When it is appropriate, follow God's calling as you embrace your vocation as God's beloved child.

Today, simply notice your life in its fullness. Effortlessly pause and open to holy moments. With wisdom and gentleness, embrace these unexpected insights, hunches, and inspirations, and expand your imagination and your love for the world in new ways.

An example of holy synchronicity in my own life involves meeting a person who eventually became my closest spiritual friend. As I was leaving a church where I had spoken, out of the corner of my eye I saw one of the participants sitting quietly in the church graveyard. Although I usually leave immediately for home after speaking engagements, *something* called me to say hello to this stranger. I am sure that this encounter was a holy moment, inspired by divine creativity and love. Had I followed my anticipated agenda, we would never have become spiritual friends. As you consider your own life plans, where do you wisely need to let go of your usual agenda to experience God's synchronous wisdom? In what new directions is God calling you through insights and synchronous encounters?

DAY 5

God Constantly Inspires Us

I will pour my spirit on all flesh;
your sons and your daughters shall prophesy,
your old men shall dream dreams,
and your young men shall see visions.

—Joel 2:28

Adventurous faith sees divine inspiration as both universal and personal and as intimate as your next breath. Every breath can be a Pentecost moment in which you join God in prayerfully healing the universe.

Divine inspiration takes many forms. Acts 2 describes the day of Pentecost dramatically in terms of a mighty wind and tongues of fire. John's Gospel describes Pentecost in terms of the less dramatic processes of holy respiration. Following the Resurrection, Jesus simply breathed on the disciples and said to them, "Receive the Holy Spirit" (John 20:22). What would it be like for you to claim the truth that with every breath, you receive the gift of God's life-transforming spirit?

The apostle Paul described God's Spirit in terms of "sighs too deep for words" (Rom. 8:26). Deep within the unconscious, God moves within our lives, quietly inspiring us to become partners in personal and global transformation. Whether you call it holy breath or divine energy, God's inspiration gives birth to and guides each moment of our lives. God's Spirit gently guides us in the direction that is best for us at the moment but leaves the details of the adventure to us. This same holy breath moved over the waters of creation (Gen. 1:1-5) and within the birth pains of the nonhuman world (Rom. 8:18-25). All things live, move, and have their being in this lively and inspiring breath of God.

As free and as ubiquitous as the wind, God's Spirit shows up everywhere, sometimes dramatically but most often in terms of subtle spiritual whispers. Even the nonhuman world breathes divine creativity, and thus, at times, subtly and synchronously guides us. "Let everything that breathes praise the LORD" (Ps. 150:6).

Every faith tradition identifies divine energy with holy breath. Words such as *chi, ki, prana, ruach, nephesh,* and *pneuma* portray the divine breath that enlivens and enlightens. Divine breath flows continually into our lives. As we claim God's inspiration, we become God's partners in sharing that life-giving breath with others. Barriers are overcome as we inhale the breath of Jesus and exhale his peace and healing into the world.

One of my spiritual mentors, Congregational minister Allen Armstrong Hunter, invited his students "to breathe the Spirit deeply in." Today, many Christians experience divine inspiration through gently breathing their "centering prayers." Buddhist spiritual guide Thich Nhat Hanh sees conscious breathing as one way we experience the spirit of peace in our lives. In words that echo the experience of Jesus' first followers when Jesus breathed upon them, the Buddhist monk counsels:

> Breathing in, I calm my body.
> Breathing out, I smile.
> Dwelling in the present moment,
> I know this is a wonderful moment![7]

Bidden or unbidden, God inspires us with every breath. New ideas, behaviors, and practices flow into our lives with each breath. Breathing within each breath, divine inspiration continually gives us all the resources we need to respond to every life situation. Pause awhile and notice God's life-giving breath in your life.

A Prayer for the Adventure

Breathe on us, divine Spirit, and give us new life. Breathe in us, Holy Wisdom, and inspire us with beauty. Breathe in every breath, so that we will know life in its abundance and share life in its wonder. Amen.

CHOOSING YOUR OWN AFFIRMATION

Breathing with God's spirit, we awaken to infinite energy, wisdom, and love. Inspiration is only a breath away. With every breath, we can experience divine peace and insight. Breathe your holy affirmations throughout the day. Take a deep breath before and after you speak or contemplate each affirmation.

- God is inspiring me with every breath.
- God inspires me as I inhale life-giving energy.
- God is inspiring me in (*a particular life situation*).
- God is inspiring me in (*a particular work situation*).

YOUR HOLY IMAGINATION

Spiritual adventure is as simple as conscious breathing. Take a moment to relax in God's presence. Gently breathe, noting each breath, slowly inhaling and exhaling. With each inhalation, say, "I breathe the Spirit deeply in." Experience the divine Spirit filling your whole being with peace and calm. Feel divine inspiration entering your life with every breath. As you exhale, send your breath into the universe with the words, "I breathe the Spirit deeply out and give it to the world again." Imagine your graceful breath contributing to the healing of the universe.

LIVING ADVENTUROUSLY

Inspiration is meant to be embodied. The Word becomes flesh; the image becomes a reality. God constantly gives you visions and images. Seeking more dramatic expressions of divine inspiration, we may miss the simple inspirations of the moment. Take time to listen to your life: What images are calling out to you? What vision is waiting to be born?

Take a small step to actualize that vision in your life today. If you consider yourself a writer or an artist, take time to write, draw, or paint each day. Julia Cameron's *The Artist's Way* provides one very creative path to release your artistic and creative gifts.[8] If you have a dream of mending the world, take time each day as you read the newspaper, listen to the radio, or watch the news to notice areas of injustice in the world. Then commit yourself to one simple, life-transforming action, such as writing your state or national representatives, joining a group such as Bread for the World or Amnesty International, sponsoring a child through a group such as Christian Children's Fund or World Vision, building a house with Habitat for Humanity, volunteering in a program that assists homeless persons or children in need, or even buying fair-trade coffee. New life and creation are just a breath away!

DAY 6

God Delights in Your Creativity

You are my Child, my beloved; with you I am well pleased.
—Mark 1:11, AP

Some Christians see God as an all-controlling sovereign who will punish us unless we do exactly as God has planned. A God who plans all the events of your life without your input is like a parent who programs a child's schedule so completely that the child has no free time simply to enjoy the leisure of a warm summer's day or read a good book just for the fun of it. Such overprogramming is hardly good parenting! Many Christians assume that any deviation from God's plan is a fall from grace that will lead to divine discipline in this life and the next. This isn't good parenting, either.

To affirm that God is adventurous is to take a radically different approach to the creative process. What if God gives us both free time and open space? What if God has a dream not only for the universe but also for the unfolding of your life? What if God's dream for your life includes many possible outcomes and invites your own input and creative spin?

I believe that God gives us space to be artists of our own experience, who contribute to God's aim at beauty in the world. While we make mistakes along the way, I believe that God is always ready to provide new opportunities for creativity, wonder, and justice seeking.

In one account of the creation of the universe, God joyfully dances with the delighted and delightful Wisdom of Life and in that dance, the world is born. This wisdom is the creative Word embodied most fully in the life of Jesus, and this Christ Wisdom is present as the animating power in our lives. Listen to God's delight in the unfolding of the universe:

> When God established the heavens, I was there,
>   when God drew a circle on the face of the deep,
> when God made firm the skies above,
>   when God established the fountains of the deep. . . .
>   then I was beside him, like a little child;[9]
> and I was daily God's delight,
>   rejoicing before the Divine always,
> rejoicing in God's inhabited world,
>   and delighting in the human race.
>   —Prov. 8:27-28, 30-31, AP

What if God seeks the same sort of delightful creative companionship for your life? I believe that God delights in the world, and God delights in you. I would like you to consider the possibility that you are created to be a cocreator in God's dream for the earth. The words God spoke to Jesus at his baptism are also addressed to you: "You are my child, my beloved; with you I am well pleased" (Mark 1:11, AP). While some Christians believe that we are so tarnished by sin that God can only love us in spite of who we are, I believe that authentic parenting, whether divine or human, involves loving each child *because* of who he or she is. Today God loves you because of who you are.

Yes, God loves you. God delights in your creativity and is inspiring you to do something beautiful for your family and your community. Just as divine creativity is motivated by love and delight, so our own creativity is meant to give joy and beauty to those around us. God wants us to be ecstatic in our creativity. God wants us to be playful like the birds of the air, colorful like the lilies of the field, and innovative like a child building a sand castle on the beach. God wants us to embrace the world in all its wonder and delight. God intends our holy play to be our gift to the universe in our place and time. God accepts the unique gifts and limitations of our lives, weaving them together with the gifts of creation to bring forth beauty in every moment of life.

A Prayer for the Adventure

Playful God, who delights in all creation and whose wisdom mothers forth the universe, let your wisdom-spirit dwell in us, inspiring us to dance and play and create in wonder and beauty and love. With wisdom as our companion, let us midwife your vision of what life can be for us, our neighbors, the stranger, and this surprising and diverse world. Amen.

CHOOSING YOUR OWN AFFIRMATION

Many of us need to experience healing in our relationship with God. We need to let go of destructive, stifling images of God and ourselves in order to embrace the gifts of divine creativity. In presenting an alternative vision of God, today's affirmations remind us that God is more loving and supportive than we can imagine. They also remind us how creative we can become as God's beloved sons and daughters. Feel free to be inventive with these affirmations in ways that reflect your own experience of God's Holy Adventure.

- God delights in my creativity.
- God loves me just as I am. I am God's beloved child.
- God delights in (*a particular gift or quality I possess*).
- My life brings beauty to everyone I meet.
- My life brings beauty to (*a particular person or situation*).

YOUR HOLY IMAGINATION

The Gospels tell the story of the generosity of a child whose gift of five loaves and two fish fed a multitude. In today's exercise in holy imagination, reflect on God's multiplication of your gifts in order to bring beauty and wholeness to yourself, those around you, and the universe.

Relax gently in a comfortable chair or lie down in a comfortable position. When you are settled, imagine that you are sitting in a great crowd of people that has come to hear the teacher Jesus. You can't wait to hear him speak. Who has come with you? Envision the crowd, your companions, and the overall environment. Take a moment to visualize Jesus as he moves through the crowd: What does he look like? What does he say to the crowd? How do you feel as you hear what he says?

As Jesus concludes his message to the crowd, he asks each member of the assembled group to bring forward his or her unique offering to help feed the multitude. How do you feel when Jesus makes this request? At first, no one moves. Then imagine yourself standing up and walking toward Jesus, with your basket in hand. What food or drink do you bring to feed the multitude?

Visualize yourself placing your lunch in Jesus' hands, and observe him praying. And, then, to your surprise, your gift is multiplied so that everyone shares in your bounty. How do feel as your simple gifts are multiplied to feed the multitude?

Now, looking at your life today: What humble gifts do you bring to "feed" the world? Visualize yourself bringing these gifts to Jesus. Experience Jesus' great delight in receiving your gifts. How do you feel as you experience God's graceful multiplication of your gifts? Experience God's abundance and generosity working in your life.

As you conclude this meditation, give thanks for God's creativity in your life.

LIVING ADVENTUROUSLY

Throughout the day, take a few moments to experience God's delight in your life in all its possibilities and apparent limitations. Then, in the spirit of the movie *Pay It Forward*, express your delight in your gifts and the gifts of those around you as they are being multiplied by God. Notice the wonder and beauty of their lives and their simple, yet vital, contributions to the universe. If it is appropriate, share your delight, gratitude, or appreciation for something another has done to enrich your life. What would it be like if words of praise and affirmation constantly characterized your relationships with God, those you know well, and strangers?

DAY 7

God's Surprising Love

God proves [God's] love for us in that while we still were sinners, Christ died for us.

—Romans 5:8

In a world in which images of divine punishment for every human imperfection were the norm, the apostle Paul challenged the norm with the affirmation "God proves [God's] love for us in that while we still were sinners, Christ died for us." While the meaning of Jesus' death remains a topic of great debate among theologians, I believe that the ultimate meaning of the cross of Jesus is God's willingness to experience our suffering, sin, and imperfection in order to heal our lives and the world. Jesus' death on the cross assures us that God is present at the place of our greatest pain, gently healing our wounds of body, mind, spirit, and relationships, regardless of their origin.

The word *sin* is not popular today in progressive, liberal, and mainstream Christian circles. Still, I believe that this ancient word needs to be reclaimed as a symbol of our personal and planetary imperfection. A beautiful planet, created in divine love and original goodness, is marred by self-interest, addiction, injustice, narcissism, racism, sexism, homophobia, and violence. Even when we seek to avoid them, we often perpetuate the social and family imperfections into which we were born through our often unconscious treatment of our children, spouses, and strangers.

The essential beauty of the universe makes our individual and social imperfections all the more tragic. In the interdependent ecology of life, we cannot escape the consequences of our own or others' alienation from God's dream for our lives and our planet. Breaking free from the impact of our own and society's imperfections is virtually impossible without God's grace embodied in healing partnerships. While we can take steps toward wholeness through commitment to an ongoing adventure of self-examination, forgiveness, and spiritual growth, the fact is that we cannot do this on our own. We need God's transforming grace working in our personal lives and through the support and accountability of a community of spiritual friends and guides in order to enable us to turn from our habitual behaviors toward the healing light of God. Our journey may require psychotherapy, medication, and spiritual guidance. But it always requires repentance, the conscious moving from one path of life to another.

Above all else, we need God's grace to liberate and inspire us when we feel we least deserve it. Grace gives us imaginative glimpses of the path ahead and the bursts of insight and energy that enable us to experience God's love and our blessedness more fully.

When many of us confront our personal imperfections, we assume that God can no longer love us. Our guilt at our imperfection, combined with feelings of unworthiness and shame, can fill us with fear and narrow our vision of divine possibilities for our lives. We see ourselves as unworthy of divine or human love. At such moments, we need to affirm that the adventurous God is also the all-loving God. God loves us eternally, unconditionally, and passionately, regardless of any blocks we might throw up. While we may block the embodiment of God's possibilities in our lives by our thoughts and behaviors, we can never completely block God's love for us. God's grace is more persistent and faithful than our temporary waywardness.

I invite you to take some time today to meditate on three of Jesus' most beloved parables, found in Luke 15. The parables of the lost sheep, lost coin, and lost sons (the latter is more commonly known as the parable of the prodigal son) portray God's unconditional love for lost persons. Read the stories slowly and attentively, letting them soak in. Which of these parables speaks most directly to your life today? In what ways might you be lost? In what ways is God reaching out to save you? Whether or not you recognize it, God is always seeking your wholeness.

Regardless of how we or others got into our current mess, God stands ready to respond with loving care. In fact, even when you are farthest from God and your deepest self, God is already sustaining you and aiming you toward nourishment, health, and well-being. Right now, God is providing the persons and events that will lead you homeward. You are loved, you are forgiven, and you are guided toward wholeness—regardless of your life situation. God loves you eternally—you were born into God's loving arms, and those arms will embrace and guide you every step of the way.

A Prayer for the Adventure

God of surprising love, awaken us to your holy adventure in our daily adventures. Help us to pause and take notice of your synchronous presence in all things. Help us to discover those holy moments in which our smallest actions may be the answer to another's deepest prayer. Help us to be attentive to graceful encounters that feed and sustain our spirits. Let us, with all creation, breathe your adventurous love. In Christ's name. Amen.

CHOOSING YOUR OWN AFFIRMATION

We say yes to God in many ways. One way is by transforming our minds through affirmations that remind us of God's constant care for us and the world. These life-transforming affirmations, when repeated regularly throughout the day, change our vision of the world and make our theology come alive.

- God loves me completely, regardless of what I have thought or done.
- God forgives my mistakes and helps me begin again.
- God is helping me find the best path in my life.
- God is liberating me from (*a particular limitation, addiction, or alienation*).

YOUR HOLY IMAGINATION

Meditatively read the story of the lost sheep from Luke 15 in terms of your life today. Let your imagination roam. Imagine that it is a dark night and you decide to go for a walk in the woods, with only starlight to guide you. Take a moment to enjoy the quiet of the evening as you wander farther and farther from camp.

When you decide to turn around, you discover that you have completely lost your bearings. You are unsure which path leads homeward. You begin to notice the sounds of wild and possibly dangerous beasts. Their nocturnal cries become louder and louder. How do you feel—lost and alone in the wilderness? How might you find your way home?

In the darkness, you hear a familiar voice—the still, small voice of God's presence—calling your name. Hear your protector and guide calling your name over and over. How do you feel when you hear your name being called? How do you respond? Do you answer? Do you cry out, "Here I am!"?

Your guide and protector emerges from the darkness. Perhaps it is Jesus. Take time to see in your mind's eye the one who is now present as your companion homeward. Your companion walks beside you, pointing out familiar landmarks. Once you've found your bearings, your companion even invites you to chart the course toward home.

Take a few minutes to journey home with your companion. Experience your companion's care but also her or his willingness for you also to become a guide on the way home.

LIVING ADVENTUROUSLY

A popular slogan proclaims, "Think globally and act locally." While there is no clear boundary between giver and receiver, we are called to bring beauty into one another's lives and provide for those who are in greatest need—whether in body, mind, and spirit, or in terms of relationships, political power, or economic justice.

Explore ways that you can become active in promoting greater well-being for persons across the planet, especially those who have lost their homes and livelihoods due to natural disasters and political upheavals. You may choose to make a contribution to international or national disaster relief through your denomination or a local project through your congregation or council of churches. You may decide to take a week off to rebuild a home that has been leveled by a hurricane or other natural disaster.

In every city there are "lost" persons—children born into poverty; persons with addictions; residents of nursing homes; persons who are mentally, physically, and emotionally homeless. As you listen to your own life, where are you called to share God's love through healing relationships with homeless, abused, and unemployed persons? As you share your gifts, what wisdom can you gain by listening to their stories and receiving their own giftedness into your own life?

In the course of every day, we have countless encounters. We meet most persons in purely pragmatic contexts—bank tellers, supermarket clerks, servers at the local coffee house. We usually know these persons only on a superficial level. Although typically these persons have virtually no power to shape the policy of their companies, these persons are nevertheless at the front line of abusive comments and judgments. So, I invite you to take time, as you did earlier this week, to look at these persons with new eyes. Assume that they are trying to do the best they can but are weighed down by heavy burdens. Without letting go of your own needs for customer service and respect, commit yourself to treating everyone you encounter, especially customer service persons, with respect and care. Even if you must assert your right to receive appropriate redress for a problem, let love and understanding color your assertiveness.

While I am not a fan of unsolicited phone calls and do my best to screen them, I have made it a point to politely decline the invitations of phone solicitors and then bid them a good day. These everyday encounters are undramatic, but you never know when they may be the "tipping point" between joy and sorrow, and health and wholeness, for those we encounter.

COMPANIONS IN THE HOLY ADVENTURE

A psychotherapist friend of mine asks the following questions on his personal answering machine, "Who are you? And what do you want?" and then cautions the unsuspecting caller, "Now, wait a moment. Be careful how you answer."

Elie Wiesel notes that "God made man because he loves stories."[1] I would add that God created the universe in all of its splendor, from the 470.4-trillion-mile-long DNA-shaped double-helix nebula to angelic hosts and currently unknown cosmic life forms and the double-helix shape of our own DNA, because God loves lively, surprising, and creative adventures. On planet Earth, we are called to be God's most lively and innovative companions in God's evolving holy adventure.

God loves a story. God loves your story. While we may gain a great deal of pleasure and escape from reading novels and the historical biographies of others, our own personal stories can be just as filled with drama, suspense, and surprising twists. How our stories will end is never entirely clear! Inspired by God, we are constantly choosing our own adventures. Sadly, we often forget the wisdom of the affirmation "God is the circle whose center is everywhere and whose circumference is nowhere."

You are centered in God, and God is calling you to play your part in the vast cosmic adventure, lived out one moment at a time, because from the very beginning we were created to be evolving, lively, and multifaceted beings whose ultimate joy is found in loving relatedness toward God, our human companions, and our fellow adventurers on planet Earth. This is what it means when the biblical tradition speaks of humankind being created by God in "our" image.

Our personal purposes are part of God's greater vision for our planet, the realization of healing and wholeness, God's shalom, in the human and nonhuman world. The prophetic vision of God, embodied in the healer Jesus, involved good news for the whole earth and for children, lambs, and lions living in God's peaceable realm. As we seek to explore God's dream for this moment as well as our lifetime, we are guided by the apostle Paul's image of the "body of Christ," whose life embraces the earth in addition to our own families, communities of faith, and all other persons of faith. In the dynamic interconnectedness that characterizes the body of Christ, we shape one another by our actions, words, emotions, and commitments. Our joys and sorrows are one. We find personal and community wholeness in expanding our local self-interest to embrace the whole earth as well as the unfolding universe in which we dwell. The glory of God, as the early Christian spiritual guide Irenaeus once proclaimed, is a human being who is fully alive and growing within the dynamic body of Christ. We are most fully alive when we claim our personal adventure as a partnership with God's moment-by-moment vision for our lives and all creation.

During this second week of your holy adventure, I invite you to take another step in recognizing who you are and discovering the deepest desires of your heart. With each step, you will discover your identity as God's beloved child, called to bring light and love to the world. Your life will be transformed so that you might know the mind of Christ as your moral and spiritual compass in your own surprising adventure. In the words of Martin Luther, you will discover that you are a "little Christ" who finds your joy in growing in wisdom and stature and relationship with God and humankind.

Take time to become more attentive to divine synchronicity and the wonders of God's holy adventure reflected in each moment and encounter.

DAY 8

You Are Created in God's Image

Then God said, "Let us make humankind in our image, according to our likeness."

—Genesis 1:26

The creation story, described in Genesis 1:1-2:4, roots our lives in God's constant and all-encompassing creativity. Everything God creates in the evolving universe shares in God's wisdom and goodness. Although humans are children of the universe with a unique planetary vocation, we are also deeply embedded in the dynamic ecology of life in all its complexity and abundance. Apart from the ambient universe of stars, seas, vegetation, and animal life, humanity would neither exist nor have a planetary home. Our well-being is connected with the well-being of rain forests, plankton, polar bears, and spotted owls. Even the humble dung beetle contributes to the well-being of the ecosystem upon which our lives depend!

We have been created in God's image, male and female. We have been created to be adventurers in God's holy adventure, celebrating and guiding our planet's evolution. Like the God who gives us birth, we experience the fullness of our calling in partnership, rather than in alienation, from the created world.

The Genesis vision of the image of God in humankind is purposely vague. While God's image is implanted in all things, we are invited to celebrate and explore our unique gifts and qualities as human beings. No one definition of the divine image is complete or final. Rather, our whole beings, bodies, minds, spirits, relationships, and communities reflect God's constant and loving artistry. Each moment incarnates God's creative word, spoken through ourselves and all creation. We "live and move and have our being" (Acts 17:28) as reflections of divine wisdom, creativity, and holiness.

There is a virtue in the vagueness of the Genesis passage "Let us make humankind in our image, according to our likeness." To define God's image too precisely leads to categorizing some persons as less than fully human if they do not meet our definition of God's presence or human uniqueness. The divine image is not restricted to intelligence, reason, or creativity but is God's ever-flowing love and light embodied in every moment of life. Regardless of our health condition, level of rationality, or even consciousness, we are the reflections of God's intimate care and loving presence. Even the "least of these" among us has a vocation to reveal God's dream for her or his particular time and place. This can never be lost!

The image of God—the light and love of Christ—within us reflects God's continual affirmation that it is "good" that we exist, that we are loved, and that we have a special place in God's holy adventure.

A Prayer for the Adventure

Bright Shining Light, whose love brings forth universes, galaxies, solar systems, and this earth, shine brightly in my heart. Let your light shine in me with passion and creativity. Let your vision transform my vision and liberate my imagination of the new world that we are creating together with your grace. Amen.

CHOOSING YOUR OWN AFFIRMATION

In the course of many years as a spiritual guide, I have found that the most difficult place for many persons to claim God's presence is in their own lives. They see themselves as unworthy of being "little Christs" to others, when, in fact, God's love and guidance are working through them each moment of their lives. Holy affirmations invite us to claim with both joy and humility our personal wholeness as reflections of divine love and light, regardless of our life situation. In affirming God's image reflected in and through our own lives, we open the door to discovering who we truly are. As you repeat today's affirmations, see yourself in a new light, and claim your identity as God's beloved child of love and light.

- I am created in God's image.
- (*Name another person*) is created in God's image.
- My life reveals God's light and love.
- I experience God's light and love in (*name a particular aspect of your own life*).

YOUR HOLY IMAGINATION

In today's imaginative prayer, simply enjoy "playing" with whatever images emerge, knowing that even our wildest images reflect God's playful dreams for our lives.[2] Take a few minutes to read meditatively the creation account from Genesis 1:1-2:4, focusing on the passage related to God's image in humankind. Reflect playfully and creatively on your images of the creating God. How do you imagine God creating this universe? Do your images reveal God as an artist, splashing forth galaxies, solar systems, and planets on the canvas of the universe? Can you visualize God as a mother or father lovingly nurturing planet Earth and the birth of humankind? Can you visualize our beloved Parent lovingly bringing forth the human race? Where do you see traces of God in the unfolding human adventure? Imagine them bursting forth in the evolving human journey. Then, in this present moment, see God's creativity and love bursting forth in your life in diverse ways, bringing forth your particular gifts. Imagine God nurturing your unique personal gifts and setting you free to create in new partnerships with God and all creation.

Conclude by thanking God for God's never-ending, loving, and all-encompassing creativity revealing itself in your active imagination. If you have not found new images today, thank God that you have positive and inspiring biblical images to be your sure foundation.

You may choose to use watercolors or draw your vision of divine creativity as a way of celebrating your faithful imagination as it opens you to new dimensions of God's imaginative presence in your life and the world.

Living Adventurously

Today, take time to expand your visions of God's image to include every person you meet. As you greet each person during the day, remind yourself to see God's image embodied in her or his life. In situations of potential conflict, take time to look deep within the other to intuit the divine image as you affirm God's image in your own life. Affirm the divine presence of love and light within her or him even when you must stand up for your principles or personal worth.

DAY 9

God's Light Shines in Your Life

The true light, which enlightens everyone, was coming into the world.
—John 1:9

I believe that the Bible is intended to be a book of vision and promise. Grounded in the dynamic and evolving interplay of unique individuals, communities of faith, historical settings, and divine inspiration, the Bible gives us many life-transforming visions of God and ourselves and challenges us to experience God's holy adventure in our own lives and communities. Divine revelation did not end with the closing of the biblical canon or a chosen set of scriptural texts. In the unfolding of God's holy adventure, we can experience divine inspiration in every moment and share our experiences with others in nonexclusive ways. We can, in the spirit of my wife's congregation's confirmation classes, write our own gospels and describe how God has made a difference in our lives and communities. God is still creating in our world and in our lives, and God calls upon us to do new and unexpected things. We are the Esthers, Pauls, Marys, Josephs, Peters, and Mary Magdalenes of our time.

Every time we pick up the Bible, we may experience a new and fresh word as the words of scripture confront our own complex, challenging, ambiguous, and wonderful world. We may even experience a radical insight that changes our lives completely.

I believe that the wisdom of Jesus' words in the Sermon on the Mount (Matt. 5–7) still shines in our time. Perhaps the boldest affirmation is Jesus' description of the true identity and task of his followers. This word enlightened Peter, James, and John, and Mary Magdalene. May it enlighten you today.

> You are the light of the world. A city built on a hill cannot be hidden. No one after lighting a lamp puts it under the bushel basket, but on the lamp-stand, and it gives light to all in the house. In the same way, let your light shine before others, so that they may see your good works and give glory to your Father in heaven (Matt. 5:14-16).

What does it mean for you to claim today that you are the light of the world? What does it mean to say that your essential vocation is to shine so brightly that others may discover God's holy light within themselves? It is not arrogant to say that you share in the light of Jesus, who is described as by John's Gospel as "the light of the world." That's what Jesus himself says about you. So let the light of Christ shine brightly within you.

As we continue in God's holy adventure, we discover that letting our light shine is a matter of vocation and service, not pride. Sadly, we often forget our identity as God's light in the world, and we let ourselves live by fear, defensiveness, guilt, and scarcity. Though we may doubt our abilities and hide our gifts, God's light still shines, constantly illuminating and transforming our lives even when we are unaware of its power.

As a child I sang, "This little light of mine, I'm gonna let it shine . . . . Everywhere I go, I'm gonna let it shine . . . Let it shine, let it shine, let it shine." I still sing this song today to remind myself that the smallest glimmer of light dispels our nighttime fears and allows us to walk in safety and confidence. God's light radiates from within our lives, and there is nothing we can do about it. We have the ability to let our light shine in varying degrees of brightness, color, and shape, for our own health and well-being and that of others as well.

A Prayer for the Adventure

Shine brightly, Holy Light; shine brightly in my life. Let your light in my light burst forth, warming my heart and the hearts of all I meet. Let every breath be praise and every word be love. In Christ's holy name I pray. Amen.

CHOOSING YOUR OWN AFFIRMATION

Though they may seem overly optimistic when we begin to use them, affirmations help us to gradually claim and express our true nature as God's children of light and love. Practicing daily affirmations sheds light on our path that enables us to experience the world and ourselves with new vision and grow into the stature that is God's intention for our lives. Today's affirmations invite you to claim your identity as God's shining lights in the world and see this same light in all of creation. Jesus says, "You are the light of the world! Let your light shine!" Look in the mirror right now and affirm with gratitude and joy, "I am the light of the world. I am shining for God!"

- I am the light of the world. I shine for God.
- You are the light of the world, _____ (*affirm another person*).
- God's light shines in my life.
- God's light shines in (*a particular person's*) life.

YOUR HOLY IMAGINATION

Robert Louis Stevenson tells the story of boys who sneak out of their homes in the darkness of night in order to meet at their clubhouse. As they venture into the darkness, each one has a lantern hidden beneath his coat. To avoid detection, they hide their lights until they reach their destination. In the safety of their meeting place, they open their coats and let their lanterns shine.[3] Whether or not others notice it, they are also children of light, and so are you!

In today's imaginative prayer, we will focus on God's light shining in us and in the world. Begin your meditation in a comfortable position, breathing gently and mindfully, deep into your belly. When you feel comfortable, imagine God's healing and transforming light entering you with each breath. Become aware of the light illumining your mind and heart, awakening your spirit, and then filling your body from the top of your head to the bottom of your feet. Experience yourself as a reflection and conduit of God's holy light flowing through you. Where is your light shining? Visualize this holy light shining from you to illuminate a particular situation in your life. See yourself as God's companion in bringing light, healing, and transformation to this situation. Imagine the persons or institutions involved, and visualize God's light flowing forth through you to enliven and enlighten them, and filling them and their environment with healing energy. Experience God's light joining all of you in a peaceful, healing environment.

Conclude by thanking God for the invitation to be a companion in sharing God's healing and illuminating presence in the world.

LIVING ADVENTUROUSLY

Seeing the light in yourself and others has personal and political implications. The early Quakers believed that God's inner light was the deepest reality of all persons. This insight led them to oppose slavery and war, treat Native Americans with respect and fairness, and champion prison reform. If you truly see and affirm the holy light in others, you must treat them in a holy manner. In our time, Mahatma Gandhi, Martin Luther King Jr., Nelson Mandela, and Desmond Tutu were inspired by their vision of God's light and presence in themselves, their people, and their adversaries to seek nonviolent social transformation.

Throughout the day, make a commitment to experience the world from the perspective of God's holy light. Look for the hidden light in everyone you meet. While you can never fully experience the inner gifts of others, take a moment in each situation to see yourself as a partner with God in bringing forth God's light in those you meet. In every encounter, seek to be God's partner in enlightening the world, subtly and gently, as a way of bringing wholeness and joy to those you meet. In every encounter, pause for a moment and take notice of God's presence in another, and then act as if you are in the presence of holiness.

Remember that the world is transformed one moment and one encounter at a time. Your light sharing and light finding in the most unlikely places may be a tipping point in others' holy adventures as well as your own.

DAY 10

You Are Growing in Wisdom and Stature

Jesus grew in wisdom and in stature, and in favor with God and humankind.

—Luke 2:52, AP

Luke's Gospel tells the colorful story of Jesus' theological and spiritual adventures in the Jerusalem temple. According to the story, Jesus was so caught up in discussing the faith of his people with the temple rabbis that he "forgot" to go home with his parents. Instead, for three whole days he listened and asked questions of the religious teachers, completely immersed in the wisdom of his faith tradition. The story concludes with Luke's commentary, "Jesus grew in wisdom and in stature, and in favor with God and humankind" (Luke 2:52, AP).

Faithful and adventurous living integrates inner and outer spiritual growth and ethical action. The first step in any adventure begins with imagining unexplored frontiers. It is obvious from Luke's Gospel that even Jesus needed to grow in his relationship with God. He needed to claim, and then push beyond, the deepest spiritual experiences of his people. The Gospels suggest that Jesus continued to grow spiritually throughout his life. Jesus constantly explored new possibilities of God's presence in his ministry of healing and transformation, and we need to do the same.

Stature is a word we don't hear often anymore. *Stature* relates to the size of your personal universe and your ability to embrace greater and greater complexity of experience without losing your personal center. The Gospels suggest that Jesus grew in stature throughout his ministry. In an encounter with a foreign woman who sought healing for her daughter, Jesus initially appeared to exclude this woman and her daughter from his circle of concern (Matt. 15:21-28; Mark 7:24-30). But in the course of the conversation, the foreign mother's faith and persistence convinced Jesus that divine healing is available to everyone. As a result of this holy encounter, Jesus grew in his embrace of ethnic diversity and in his understanding of the scope of his mission. We too are called to goad one another gently and supportively so that we might also grow in wisdom and stature in our own embrace of diversity in the church and the world.

The Orthodox Christian tradition speaks of "divinization" as the unending process of embodying God's presence in our lives. Today's global Christians are challenged to imagine ourselves as persons of great stature as we lovingly embrace the pluralism of our time. As we deepen our relationship with God and grow in stature, we transcend narrow parochialisms and stifling fundamentalisms, and make friends with the dynamic complexity of life. We will discover the many faces of God in learning about the world's many spiritual traditions. We can also embrace our own personal complexity in our quest for personal wholeness and spiritual understanding. As we grow in wisdom and stature, our own personal adventures become global and cosmic pilgrimages as our personal stories join with the Holy Adventure that inspires and undergirds wisdom seeking everywhere. Whether or not you are aware of it, the universe and planet are still evolving, and that same evolutionary energy and love are calling you to become Christlike in your love and stature.

A Prayer for the Adventure

Artist of Creation, bringing forth planets of beauty and persons of stature, help us, like the Teacher of Nazareth, to commit ourselves to growing in your wisdom and stature. Awaken us to experience all creation as holy, and all creatures as companions on this good earth. Expand our circle of concern, and energize us to acts of mercy and justice. Let us, by your wisdom and grace, do something beautiful for you, O God. Amen.

CHOOSING YOUR OWN AFFIRMATION

Throughout this holy adventure, I have pointed out the importance of simple awareness, or mindfulness, in the spiritual adventure. It can begin with simple acts of pausing and noticing what's going on in our hearts and minds, and then opening to deeper truths about ourselves and the world. Curiosity and self-examination are essential to spiritual growth. Certain holy affirmations help us widen our attention and sensitivity. Such affirmations challenge us to wake up to the opportunities for transformation and adventure in our own experience and beyond in our widening circle of encounters. While synchronous moments awaken us to new possibilities, true spiritual growth is never accidental but arises from our ongoing commitment to embrace greater dimensions of reality within and beyond our personal lives. Today, in this spirit, I invite you to claim the following affirmations:

- I am continually growing in wisdom and stature.
- I embrace diversity and complexity with love and understanding.
- I welcome God's wisdom in (*a particularly complex situation*).
- I embrace God's call to growth in (*a situation of diversity or pluralism*).

YOUR HOLY IMAGINATION

Take some time to read meditatively the story of Jesus in the temple as if it is your own story. Imagine yourself coming to a holy place in search of wisdom and stature. You want a greater sense of God's purpose in the world and in your life. What holy place have you chosen? Imagine your holy place—experience its unique spirit; bathe in its inspiration. (It might be a cathedral or chapel, library or seminary, a beach or mountain lake.)

In the course of your contemplation, you discover that you are not alone—the divine teacher Jesus (or someone who reveals God's wisdom to you) has joined you. What does the teacher say to you? What is your initial response to her or him?

You enter into dialogue with the teacher. What questions do you ask? How does the teacher respond? What is your reply to the teacher's words?

As you conclude your conversation, I invite you to ask one more question of Jesus: "Where do I need to grow spiritually in my life today?" Listen deeply to God's wisdom in your life. What does the teacher say in response? What do you learn from the encounter?

As the teacher bids you farewell, take time to give thanks for God's wisdom within your life. (If no new insights emerged during your time of imaginative prayer, take time to reflect on ways you might tap the divine wisdom in your life.)

LIVING ADVENTUROUSLY

Growing in wisdom and stature involves embracing diversity in terms of both ideas and persons. Our spiritual adventures call us constantly to expand and deepen our circles of relatedness and ethical concern. Our affirmations take shape in creative encounters with "otherness." As you look at your intellectual circle, what new concepts or ideas might you need to consider? What important but neglected insights might you need to explore? What one commitment might you make today in order to expand your intellectual, ethical, and spiritual horizons?

For example, following 9/11, many Christians committed themselves to explore the Islamic tradition in its many diverse forms. Through this search, they discovered common ground in the Abrahamic covenant that joins Jews, Christians, and Muslims. Some explored more deeply the diverse and healthy resources of their own faith as they explored the diversity and wisdom of the other's faith. They committed themselves to see Islam in terms of its eternal and inspiring truths rather than in terms of its fundamentalist factions.

In my own family life, during the week following 9/11, we made it a point to eat dinner at a neighborhood restaurant owned by an Iraqi family. After our meal, we expressed our concern and support for them and told them where to reach us if any problems arose for which they might need support and help. We were greeted with gratitude and appreciation, and a row of smiling faces peeking out from the kitchen, along with a special dessert!

As you look at your own life, who are the persons that lie beyond your typical circle of concern? How might you make a commitment to expand your circle of concern to include these persons and explore ways to engage them as companions on your common spiritual journey?

DAY 11

You Can Grow Through Consciously Confronting Life's Temptation

[Jesus] was in the wilderness for forty days, experiencing temptation, and he was with wild beasts; and angels waited on him.
—Mark 1:13, AP

As God's messenger to humankind, Jesus experienced the fullness of human life, including conflict and temptation. Our own journey from childhood to maturity also involves discovering that life is complicated and that our greatest gifts can be the source of our greatest temptations.

Theologians often speak of the human adventure as ambiguous, both personally and socially. Nuclear radiation enables us to diagnose and treat cancer, yet nuclear weapons can threaten the existence of the human race. Further, nuclear wastes threaten the long-term ecological stability of our planet. Medical technology relieves pain and lengthens our lives; but patients can become victims of this technology when the spiritual, emotional, and relational aspects of medicine and health are forgotten.

Spiritual leaders remind us that the closer we come to experiencing God's holy adventure, the more obvious our imperfections become to us. As imperfect, evolving, and inspired children of God, we are constantly discovering that as we embrace greater complexity and creativity, we also experience greater challenge and temptation. These temptations are not directly sent by God to test our character but are the natural result of our personal growth and our openness to growing in stature and vocation.

The story of Jesus' temptations in the desert reminds us that Jesus faced challenges similar to ours today. On the day of his baptism, Jesus heard God's affirmation of his life: "You are my beloved Son." This life-changing mystical event undoubtedly inspired Jesus to seek his vocation as a healer, Spirit-filled person, and teacher. However, Jesus had to journey beyond the comfort of his previous religious experiences in order to claim God's holy adventure in his own life. In the wilderness, Jesus knew both divine intimacy and personal temptation. He had to confront the totality of his experience, including temptation, ambivalence, and fear in order to bring healing to the struggles and complexities of human life.

Jesus faced the temptations of comfort, power, and safety. He could have become a leader of nations with the goal of restoring Israel to its ancient glory. He could have been absolutely safe regardless of the threat. He could have enjoyed complete physical well-being and satisfaction. Jesus' adventure in the wilderness reminds us that typically we are not tempted by bad things but by good things that stand in the way of living God's dream for our lives. As Nikos Kazantzakis suggests in *The Last Temptation of Christ*, Jesus knew the allure and positive values inherent in comfort, safety, and romance. But had he followed the path of domestic tranquillity rather than the way of the Cross, we would have never known the full extent of the saving power of God's light and love to conquer all things, even death.

Jesus shows us that spiritual maturity involves claiming the whole of our lives and discovering divine wisdom in life's temptations and complexities.

Claiming God's holy adventure also involves risking our own personal safety and achievements in order to commit ourselves to the healing of the planet and our closest companions.

As the story of Jesus' prayer in the garden of Gethsemane notes, the Savior of humankind experienced temptation throughout his ministry. At the crossroads, when he could choose long life or the way of the Cross, Jesus clearly struggled to follow his deepest vocation. He did not want to die. Nor do I believe that God foreordained his death. But in his moments of life-and-death decision making, Jesus chose the way of the Cross as the fulfillment of his vocation as God's healer and teacher. The words "Father, if you are willing, remove this cup from me; yet, not my will but yours be done" point to Jesus' willingness, within his own quest for spiritual stature, to align himself with God's passion to heal and transform humankind (Luke 22:42).

While our own struggles are seldom as complex and life-transforming as Jesus' wilderness experience, we also are called to place the complexities of our lives in the context of God's wider visions for us and the well-being of others. In our own time, Martin Luther King Jr. had a magnificent dream of wholeness and justice for America, and he knew that he might not make it to the promised land of freedom for all Americans. No doubt he had other options than taking the fateful trip to Memphis, Tennessee, some of which involved comfort and economic prosperity. Yet, embracing his vocation as a spiritual leader for his time, King chose to face his fears and find God in the midst of the struggle for justice for sanitation workers, even though assassination loomed as a distinct possibility.

On your journey as a companion in God's holy adventure today, I invite you to hold Jesus as your model for facing the complexities and temptations that accompany your spiritual growth. His temptations, like ours, were real. He found healing, direction, and wholeness amid temptation by praying about his temptations, and you can too. When you must make a major life-changing decision or struggle between good and better options or choose between taking the easy or the challenging spiritual path, I invite you to pause and intentionally place your life in God's care. Share your struggles with the one "unto whom all hearts are open and all desires are known" and let God's wisdom, love, and light guide you to do what is best for yourself and others.

A Prayer for the Adventure

Heart of the universe, who knows me better than I know myself, I thank you for your guiding presence in my life. Lure me toward wholeness. Inspire me to face the heights and depths of life, to explore all that I am in its ambiguity. Let your light of truth and womb of becoming shine a light on all that I am and then bring forth fruits of the Spirit from within the garden of temptation. In the name of the Healer, Jesus. Amen.

CHOOSING YOUR OWN AFFIRMATION

Holding spiritual affirmations in your heart enables you to keep your focus on your partnership with God amid life's complexities. Affirmations enable you to discern the difference between your own self-interest and the highest possible good for yourself and those around you in any given situation. They remind you that you are never alone in the wilderness. God's Spirit is supporting and guiding you even when you are least aware of it.

- God is with me in every struggle.
- God guides me during my times of temptation.
- I pray about my temptations and listen for God's guidance.
- In (*a particular situation*), I seek God's guidance and follow God's wisdom.

YOUR HOLY IMAGINATION

Meditatively read the Gospel accounts of Jesus in the wilderness (Matt. 4:1-11; Luke 4:1-13), letting their meaning soak into your life. As you reflect on these passages, let your mind wander to a wilderness place apart from friends and family. Visualize yourself walking through this empty and apparently barren wilderness. You are there to discern your next steps in the spiritual adventure. What does the wilderness look like? How do you feel as you walk in solitude?

As you walk, you reflect on your life's vocation. Find a place to sit and take a few deep breaths. As you look at your life, what events or activities have been fulfilling to you? What were the life-giving factors in that event or activity? What holy possibilities inspire you? What spiritual dream leads you toward the vocation that will bring healing, wholeness, and joy to yourself and others? Take a moment to meditate upon your deepest vocational possibilities.

Now listen even more intently to your life as you get up and walk deeper into the wilderness. What temptations stand in the way of fulfilling your spiritual vocation? Pause again and take a few breaths; then seek a revelation of your deepest temptations, their attraction, and how following them would shape your life. Notice how you feel about your temptations.

Now, in the solitude of the wilderness, you discover you are not alone. You suddenly notice that Jesus is beside you. Take a few moments to visualize Jesus at your side. What does he look like? What is he wearing?

What thoughts and feelings do you share with Jesus? How does he respond to your concerns? What guidance does he give you?

After your exchange, both of you continue to walk through the wilderness. As you reach the edge of the wilderness, what parting words do you speak to Jesus? Hear Jesus say to you: "I am always with you. In times of struggle and temptation, just call on me. I stand beside you as your closest friend to help and guide you."

You may choose to conclude this imaginative journey with a time of thanksgiving, reflection, and journaling related to God's ever-present guidance and insight.

LIVING ADVENTUROUSLY

The complexities and the busyness of our schedules seldom give us time to reflect on our inner personal challenges from the perspective of our spiritual vocation. While our lives may be full, we need times of silence and meditation in order to gain perspective on our lives and to open to God's holy adventure within our own adventures.

I suggest that you seek your own wilderness times on a regular basis. You may choose to take a few hours of personal retreat every week, a day each month, or go away for a long weekend or week each year to take your spiritual pulse and find your vocational bearings. There are retreat centers throughout the country that provide opportunities for personal and group retreats. Your spiritual director, pastor, or denominational leader should be able to provide you with information on retreat centers where you can find resources for your wilderness explorations into your holy adventure with God.

DAY 12

Christ's Mind Is Within You

Let the same mind be in you that was in Christ Jesus.
—Philippians 2:5

While the biblical tradition is realistic about human imperfection, its primary affirmations involve the relationship between a loving and adventurous God and human beings who share in God's lively and evolving creativity. In his description of Christ's saving presence in the universe, the apostle Paul calls his listeners to claim their deepest identity in relationship to Christ: "Let the same mind be in you that was in Christ Jesus" (Phil. 2:5). We can share in Christ's mission because Christ's spirit and mind are essential to our identity. The flow of God's energy and wisdom within us gives birth to and guides each moment of our lives. Although our own moment-by-moment creativity shapes the character of God's presence in our lives, there is always a Christlike movement in our experience regardless of our attentiveness to God's vision for our lives. In Romans 8, Paul describes the deep connection between God's Spirit and our own: "When we cry, 'Abba! Father!' it is that very Spirit [of God] bearing witness with our spirit that we are children of God" (Rom. 8:15-16). God's voice speaks through every thought, emotion, and action at the deepest level of our being.

As the ever-present life force and inspiration throughout creation, the mind of Christ is not just cerebral. Today, medical scientist Candace Pert speaks of the "molecules of emotion," peptides that are present in our brains, residing throughout our bodies.[4] The quality of our thoughts and emotions influences our overall well-being. The body is inspired, and the mind is embodied. In the same way, the mind of Christ inspires every aspect of our lives, including our bodies.

> Your holy adventure bursts forth energetically as you experience the infinity and interdependence of yourself and all things within God's evolving holy adventure.

According to the apostle Paul, we experience the mind of Christ through loving connectedness (Phil. 2:5-11). What is unique about Christ, Paul asserts, is not his power or sovereignty but his humble identification with the suffering and hope of humankind. The mind of Christ allows us to see our reflection and the presence of God in all creation, and inspires us to claim our connection with our companions on the multibillion-year cosmic adventure.

Reflect a moment on the unique quality of Jesus' ministry. He saw wholeness and infinity within broken and finite people. He saw the passion of God hidden within all sorts of people—prostitutes, farmers, fishermen, revolutionaries, Roman sympathizers, and little children. This same holy passion is your deepest reality.

"There is more" to your experience and the world than you can imagine. The infinite universe takes birth in each moment of your life. The mind of Christ is growing within you. Your holy adventure bursts forth energetically as you experience the infinity and interdependence of yourself and all things within God's evolving holy adventure.

A Prayer for the Adventure

Holy Adventure, whose vision brings forth beauty in all things and sees wonders in galaxies, dancing children, fireflies, and T cells, awaken me to your vision in my life. Help me experience the world as Jesus did, hearing your voice in the wind, smelling the fragrance of love in anointing oil, experiencing healing energy in touch, tasting your goodness in meals of companionship, and seeing your wonder in the least and the lost. Bless my mind and all my senses that they might give you glory as they bless the world through thoughts, words, feelings, and acts of love. Amen.

CHOOSING YOUR OWN AFFIRMATION

Our affirmations transform the way we see the universe. Holy affirmations increase our awareness of the divine within ourselves and others. In daily claiming the reality of divine inspiration through the use of spiritual affirmations, our lives come to reflect the omnipresent wisdom of God. Even our bodies are transformed and enlivened by the impact of holy affirmations. Our own awareness of God enables God to be more active in our lives, giving us insights that we could never have experienced without our commitment to this form of spiritual growth.

- Christ's mind speaks through my mind.
- In Christ's mind, I am connected with all things.
- Christ's energy flows through my body, mind, and spirit.
- I experience Christ's wisdom in (*a particular situation*).

YOUR HOLY IMAGINATION

Today many persons have reclaimed the social gospel question "What would Jesus do?" Closely connected with this affirmation is another affirmation: "What would Jesus see?" What we see and do are intimately connected. In this exercise in holy imagination, take a few moments to relax in God's presence. Then visualize the day ahead. Whom will you meet? With whom will you work? As you visualize your day, look deep into the faces of those you anticipate meeting. Experience their deeper reality. See yourself connected with them in God's lively interdependence. Feel God's holy energy flowing from your life to theirs and back again. See God working in their lives as well as your own life. Visualize each encounter as an opportunity to grow spiritually and experience the mind of Christ.

LIVING ADVENTUROUSLY

God's holy imagination is embodied in everyday life. Commit yourself to being mindful of God's presence and ideals in your encounters today. Now put into practice what you experienced imaginatively. In your encounters throughout this day, commit yourself to seeing Christ's presence in others. Experience in these encounters the quality of interdependence that joins both of you as partners in healing the world. Let your sense of self expand to include the well-being of everyone you meet. Let your words and actions contribute to their experience of God's holy adventure in their lives. Let everything you say be guided by the mind of Christ and God's quest for healing and wholeness.

DAY 13

You Are Meant to Grow as God's Beloved Child

[Jesus said,] "Put out into the deep water and let down your nets for a catch."

—Luke 5:4

God loves stories and wants you to be a conscious participant within God's own story—God's holy adventure. While the Bible is full of commandments, counsel, and affirmations, many of us find our greatest inspiration in its stories of persons of faith who found themselves at moments of great decision that shaped countless others who came after them. In their stories, we glimpse our own story as holy adventurers. As we imaginatively place ourselves in their adventures and identify with their lives, we see our lives from a new perspective. We discover that our small decisions may not be so small after all. We wonder whether we have just entertained angels dressed in ordinary garb. We realize that despite our limitations and anonymity, our prayers, choices, and actions may be the tipping point between life and death for ourselves, a friend, and even the planet. Like the butterfly whose flapping wings along the Pacific Coast create vibrations that make the difference between a drizzle and an ice storm in New York City, our smallest, least remembered acts may bring healing to the universe. It is a joy and a challenge to remember with the Jewish mystics that, in the lively interconnectedness of life, to save one soul is to save the universe!

We are incarnations of the Divine Wisdom that has guided the universe for billions of years. Just as the universe is intended to evolve toward greater beauty and complexity, so humankind is being called over and over again to participate in God's cosmic adventure. While the holy adventure is global, it is played out in the individual stories of our lives, of persons who work day after day for world peace, to feed the hungry, and to welcome the foreigner.

Many of us can identify with Jesus' encounter with Peter, who was ready to quit after a long and unsuccessful night of fishing (Luke 5:1-11). We have worked long and hard on projects, only to have them disregarded by our supervisors or colleagues. At the peak of our professional lives, we have found ourselves downsized or passed over for a promotion. As an author, I have experienced both small and large failures. A morning's writing is wiped out by a power surge and my own neglect to save a document. A text that took months to write and reflects the best of my thinking at the time is rejected by publisher after publisher. Yes, we know what it is like to fish all night and catch nothing! At times, we want to give up, retire, retreat to the sidelines, or settle for less in life. But God calls us to go farther and deeper. God wants us to seek abundant life in deeper waters. Moment by moment, God gives us a dream and the inner passion and imagination to make it come true. The urge to go deeper and farther lures us beyond the familiarity of our known world. This urge for adventure comes from God.

For Peter and ourselves, this holy passion means believing that despite our previous failures, there is more—more to fishing, more to faith, and more to life—than we can ever imagine.

Philosopher Alfred North Whitehead once said that the conservative who wants to hold on to life as it once was goes against the essence of the universe. We can treasure the past and its achievements; we can gladly return home for high school or college reunions. But to relive them day after day would deaden our spirits. We are meant for new adventures, deeper insights, deeper waters, and an infinite journey in partnership with God.

God creates you to evolve and grow, and to see the world in new and surprising ways. It is vital that we, as partners in God's holy adventure, consciously claim the unique adventure that is ours, building on God's dreams and creating new dreams of our own.

A Prayer for the Adventure

O God, you call us to go into deeper waters. Help us to let go of past successes and failures that we might create with you the dream of tomorrow and the hope of the future. Let your imaginative love flow in and through us to give birth to the dreams that await our commitment to bring them forth. Amen.

CHOOSING YOUR OWN AFFIRMATION

Like the famous saying in *The Little Engine That Could*—"I think I can, I think I can"—our spiritual affirmations give us the energy and focus to scale heights that once seemed insurmountable. When we grow weary, we discover that the Energy of the universe moves within us to give us a second wind. In this spirit, I invite you to claim the following adventuresome affirmations:

- I am constantly growing in faith and insight.
- With God's help, I have the energy and insight to respond to any problem.
- Behind every failure, God has a placed a new dream for me.
- God inspires me with new possibilities in (*name a particular situation*).
- I courageously venture into deep waters with God as my companion.

YOUR HOLY IMAGINATION

Meditatively read Luke 5:1-11, taking time to inhale deeply its spiritual insights. When you are relaxed, place yourself in the scene described by the Gospel story. Imagine that you have been fishing all night and are returning to shore. Take a moment to visualize the environment—the sea, the land, the sky above. Visualize your fishing companions. Who are they?

Despite your skills, you have been totally unsuccessful. For all your efforts, you have caught nothing. How do you feel? What worries or concerns do you have as you return to shore?

As you look at your life, have you ever been in a similar situation? How do you feel about it today?

As you row to shore, imagine that you are met by Jesus, standing at the dock. What does he look like? How does he greet you? How do you respond when he says, "Go back out again, but this time, go deeper and farther"? Do you choose to go deeper? If you give up, what are the consequences of turning your back on God's call?

But if you choose to go deeper, imagine yourself casting your net into deeper waters. Imagine the greatest catch of your life. Imagine your net filling with fish to the breaking point. How do you feel? What do you say to Jesus when you return to the shore with your boat filled with fish?

Now look again at your own life today. Where might Jesus tell you to go deeper? What would your dream of going deeper look like? What are the consequences of giving up on this particular dream? If you choose, imagine yourself going deeper and making an abundant catch. What abundant gift would come from trusting God and yourself to take the next step of the adventure?

Conclude by seeing yourself amid your unexpected abundance and giving thanks for God's dream for your life and God's passion that you live the dream!

LIVING ADVENTUROUSLY

Your overall well-being depends on your willingness to live your dreams each day by confronting challenge and failure with hope and optimism. Today, consciously take time to launch out farther and deeper in your life's adventure. Prayerfully look for alternative ways to respond to places in your life where you perceive you have failed. Look for undiscovered places where previously you saw only scarcity. Look for places you have never "fished" before. Move farther and deeper by one small action today that may eventually lead to living God's dream for your life.

DAY 14

You Are Always Connected with God

In [God] we live and move and have our being.

—Acts 17:28

At the heart of your spiritual adventure is the affirmation that the creator God of the universe is also the personal God of your life. The theological term for this is "divine omnipresence." It simply means that God is everywhere and in everything, responding to each creature intimately and personally, from within as well as from without. Whether or not we are aware of it, we live in a divine environment, where we receive divine inspiration continually and personally.

Paul's words to the philosophical community of Athens speak to us in our own pluralistic and postmodern time—in God "we live and move and have our being." God's inspiration is the transformative force that wells up within us, gently guides our journeys, supports our creativity, and creates the center from which we improvise in the artistry of our lives. While we cannot fathom the length and breadth of the universe, we can envision God as the personal energy whose dynamic presence gives life and direction to galaxies and to ourselves.

Paul's words are especially helpful for today's spiritual adventurers. Paul invoked the wisdom of the Greek philosophical tradition to describe God's unique revelation in Jesus Christ. Though Paul was Jewish by ethnicity and Christ-centered in theology, he believed that the reality present in Christ inspires the wisdom residing within every faith tradition. Christians can embrace the insights and practices of other faiths, precisely because persons of other religious traditions also participate in the holy adventure of God's omnipresence. While we travel different paths and receive different insights from God, we are all inspired by the Holy and Loving One.

"We are God's offspring," says Acts 17:28-29. What an amazing vision. What if you were to embrace the belief that God is "birthing" you in each moment and then letting you crawl or walk at your own natural pace?

Ever changing and ever growing, God's inspiration is always aimed at wholeness, beauty, and justice for ourselves and the universe. We are constantly connected with God's vision for each moment, and this reality connects us moment by moment in healing ways with the rest of the planet and the ones with whom we are most intimate.

Today, I invite you to affirm that you are God's offspring. You are God's beloved child and live, move, and have your being in God's holy adventure. Embrace this affirmation with your every thought and experience throughout the day. Live this affirmation as you seek to affirm your connectedness with the whole of God's beloved universe.

The English mystic Julian of Norwich experienced God in a hazelnut and discovered that she was also a manifestation of God's loving artistry. In Dame Julian's words:

> [God] showed me something small, no bigger than a hazelnut, lying in
> the palm of my hand, as it seemed to me, and it was as round as a ball. I
> looked at it with the eye of my understanding and thought: What can this

be? I was amazed that it could last, for I thought because of its littleness it would have suddenly fallen into nothing. And I was answered in my understanding: It lasts and always will, because God loves it; and thus everything has being through the love of God.[5]

As you ponder God's loving creativity continuously sustaining your own life, what is your "hazelnut"? What is your reminder throughout the day that God is your constant companion and guide?

A Prayer for the Adventure

God of hazelnuts, quarks, butterflies, and galaxies, inspire us to experience all things at the center of your love and all things as divine in origin and destiny. Breathe in us, Ever-living Spirit of life and adventure, so that every breath is a prayer and blessing, every breath a healing breath for ourselves and our planet Earth. Let every breath be praise and prayer. Amen.

CHOOSING YOUR OWN AFFIRMATION

Today, take time to experience the divine environment that supports you and gives you life through the following affirmations.

- I live and move and have my being in God.
- Divine energy enlivens and inspires me throughout the day.
- The infinite energy of the universe inspires and revitalizes me.
- I experience divine energy and inspiration in (*a particular situation*).

YOUR HOLY IMAGINATION

In this imaginative prayer, visualize what it means to live and move and have your being in God. Take time simply to center yourself in God's care. With each breath become more aware of your connectedness with God. Let God's energy replenish your vitality one breath at a time.

When you feel connected and relaxed, imagine yourself moving in a vast sea of holy energy. What does this sea look like? Visualize this divine energy and inspiration palpably flowing through your life as the ultimate source of your personal inspiration and vitality. Experience it arising from every cell in your body and manifesting itself in every insightful thought. Feel this holy energy nurturing you from every direction, from within and without—through your breath, in your heartbeat, in your thoughts, and all around you.

Visualize yourself as connected with every other human being. Be aware of yourself and those you love breathing together as part of one Great Breath, nurturing and supporting one another with every inhalation.

Expand your vision one more time. Imagine the whole universe as the reflection of one great life breath of Wisdom in its many forms. Acknowledge and affirm sthat you are connected with all things in the dynamic interplay of giving and receiving the Divine Life Force.

LIVING ADVENTUROUSLY

God's holy adventure arises from the intricate interconnectedness of all things. The Spirit of God moves and breathes in all things, creating and transforming them. Today, live in the spirit of this holy interconnectedness that gives life to you and all things. As you go through the day, feel your connection with everyone you meet. Take time to sense God as the connecting force in every encounter. Pause and open yourself to experience how you nurture their lives and also receive life from them. Open your hands and heart to give and receive in every encounter. See every encounter as an opportunity to promote healing and reconciling relationships. Let God's Spirit connect you with all things.

You may choose to carry a hazelnut or prayer beads in your pocket or a cross around your neck to remind you of the divine environment within which you live. In this spirit, each member of my family wears a Celtic cross as a sign that wherever we are, we are joined in Christ. Throughout the day, I touch that cross to remind myself of the God in whom I, my loved ones, and all creation "live and move and have our being."

WEEK
3

CALLED TO PARTNERSHIP

Living fully into God's holy adventure for your life is always personal but never solitary. God wants us to experience fullness of life. As members of the body of Christ who are called to reflect the mind of Christ in all we do and say, we are meant to experience a variety of inspired and inspiring holy relationships, and we are called to claim our partnership in God's loving realm in this life and the next. In this lively and holy adventure, we are called to let our own holy and adventurous light shine upon our families, congregations, and communities, for their transformation as well as our own.

Dorotheos of Gaza, a sixth-century hermit who lived in the Egyptian desert for sixty years, once described the human adventure in terms of a circle in which each person is situated at the circumference, with God at the center. According to Dorotheos, the nearer we come to the center of the circle, the nearer we are to our brothers and sisters. On the other hand, the nearer we come to our brothers and sisters, the closer we become to God. In the words of W. H. Auden, we are called to "love God in the World of the Flesh."[1]

I believe that God calls us to love this complex, interdependent, and embodied world. For those who affirm divine omnipresence and omni-activity, earth and heaven are not in opposition to one another. God's passion for wholeness and beauty is revealed in God's loving and eternal community, and it is also incarnate in the face of your beloved, in a purring cat, in the face of a hungry child, and in the ducks flying south for the winter. This is the meaning of Jesus' best-known prayer, the "Abba prayer," in which he prayed that the Abba's will be done "on earth as it is in heaven." To be sure, our earth shares in God's vision of shalom, but this vision needs our partnership and creativity to be realized in our world.

The biblical tradition affirms the divine-human partnership in healing the world. God called women and men such as Sarah and Abraham, Ruth and Samuel, Esther and Moses, and Mary and Joseph to share in God's healing purposes and goals for history. God calls each one of us and our faith communities to share in God's dream of justice and beauty for all creation.

> Everything we do is treasured in God's everlasting life. Each act opens or closes the door to the realization of God's vision in this time and place.

Our personal adventure always has an impact on our families and communities. What if we believed that our adventure also makes a difference to God? If God experiences all things, then what we do, to a smaller or greater degree, truly matters to God, because it shapes God's experience and activity in the world. Everything we do is treasured in God's everlasting life. Each act opens or closes the door to the realization of God's vision in this time and place.

In this section, we will explore the meaning of God's call to partnership in healing the world. What does it mean to choose our own adventure and, at the same time, affirm and support the adventures of our brothers and sisters? Each day this week, I pray that you will discover that your vocation is simply to embody the words of Mother Teresa: "Do something beautiful for God."

You Are Blessed to Be a Blessing

I will bless you, and make your name great, so that you will be a blessing.

—Genesis 12:2

Y ou are blessed! You are blessed because God is constantly present in your life, giving you guidance, insight, and energy. God's holy adventure makes a way for freedom and beauty where you might otherwise imagine only a dead end. Our spiritual practices awaken us to the dynamic flow of divine love and guidance in our lives and in the world so much that in each moment of life, we can catch a glimpse of God's vision for our lives today and for the planet in the years to come. This is the glorious blessing of living in awareness of the omnipresence of God in daily life.

God cherishes our spiritual adventures in their uniqueness. Scripture describes God's unexpected blessings over and over to show us that we are also blessed, just like Abraham and Sarah. These aged adventurers were children of promise—the promise of a new land and biological descendants. Yet, although they had discovered God's guidance in the wilderness, still they had no child and were long past their childbearing years. Imagine their hopelessness and uncertainty as they pondered God's extravagant promise that their descendants would be as numerous as the stars in the sky. The child they anticipated carried the promise of a nation yet unborn.

The birth of Isaac, like the birth of Jesus centuries later, would transform the human adventure in unimaginable ways.

Like this legendary couple, we are also blessed to be a blessing in unimaginable ways. To be blessed is to experience the great joy of God's presence in your life and to know the gift of a larger perspective in which your well-being and the well-being of those who come after you are united in God's loving vision of the universe.

Blessedness may be experienced even in the darkest moments of life. That is the message of the Beatitudes (Matt. 5:1-10). Those who mourn and discover that God is their only hope are blessed. The ability to mourn is itself the gift of love. When we encounter God in the struggle for peace and justice; in experiences of grief, financial uncertainty, and personal vulnerability; and in the restless quest for an intimate encounter with the living God, we recognize God's blessing and peace that passes all understanding. In such moments, we discover that God is our unseen partner in the quest for shalom.

Blessedness is the gift of a larger perspective on our lives. Even as they struggle with their childlessness, Abraham and Sarah are challenged to look beyond their barrenness to live their daily lives in light of the generations to come. Like them, we must trust that God's dream for the immediate moment also includes the unknown and unexpected future. God's vision of your personal adventure includes those you will directly touch and those who are shaped indirectly through your blessing of others. This is the insight of the film *It's a Wonderful Life*. Driven to despair by the specter of bankruptcy, George Bailey sees his life as an exercise in futility, only to discover that by simply going about his business, his life has shaped a family, community, and nation.

Each of our actions has consequences that radiate out into the universe, shaping the lives of persons we will never meet. A simple word of gratitude can transform another person's life and create a chain reaction that will positively transform many others. A word of welcome to a stranger can awaken a sense of value and purpose that is passed on from generation to generation. Often unbeknownst to us, our prayers shape the world to come and transform the lives of others. By God's grace, living out our vocations joins our own quest for wholeness and joy with the healing of the neighborhood and the planet. Awakened to a world of blessing and wonder, we can affirm with Rabbi Abraham Joshua Heschel:

Just to be is a blessing.
Just to live is holy.

A Prayer for the Adventure

Holy One, you know where the pain and trauma are in our lives. You know the hurts we bear, the memories that burden our hearts, and the prisons of childhood pain. Remind us that you are with us in the struggle for wholeness. Remind us that our pain is your pain, and our celebration your celebration. Holy One, your healing touch rests upon us. Help us open to healing that embraces pain and transforms it to blessing. In Christ's name. Amen.

CHOOSING YOUR OWN AFFIRMATION

In the intricate interdependence of life, our lives contribute to the spiritual adventures of everyone we meet and countless persons we may never directly encounter. Affirmations enable us to experience the holy interconnectedness of life and commit ourselves to sharing God's blessings in every encounter. Choose one or more of the following affirmations, and say it to yourself several times a day.

- God blesses me so I can be a blessing.
- I bless each person I meet.
- I bless (*a particular person*).
- "Just to be is a blessing. Just to live is holy."

YOUR HOLY IMAGINATION

In the film *It's a Wonderful Life*, George Bailey receives a vision of holy interconnectedness. He discovers that his life was not a failure but a blessing to his family, friends, and community. Through his impact on his brother during their childhood, George even influenced the course of World War II. As humble as your life may be, its impact ripples across the community and the planet.

In the imaginative prayer that follows, take time to breathe deeply, relaxing in the presence of God. Let your mind wander to a point in your life in which your words or actions contributed to the long-term wholeness and well-being of another. Imagine the details of a particular moment. What did you do or say to support another person's growth and adventure? How did that person respond? How did it make a difference in her (his) life and in your own life? Were you aware of the impact at the time? Have you stayed in touch with this person? Consider contacting this person and letting her (him) know you still remember her (him).

Now, reflect on an upcoming encounter in which you may be a messenger of God's wisdom and love in another's life. Take a moment to imagine this upcoming encounter. Visualize yourself not worrying about the details of the encounter but simply being open to how you can support another person's holy adventure.

Conclude with a moment of thanksgiving for the many encounters through which you have been blessed to be a blessing.

LIVING ADVENTUROUSLY

You truly are blessed to be a blessing. Giving and receiving blessings is both a matter of intentionality and awareness. Often we don't see something if we aren't intentionally looking for it. In contrast, it is my experience that once we commit ourselves to a spiritual path, we are immediately made aware of countless opportunities to embody that path in our everyday lives. These opportunities were always present as possibilities in our personal adventure, but our own awareness allows us to participate consciously in the full circle of blessings given to us daily.

Today, experiment with making a commitment to bless everyone you meet. You can do this with a short prayer at every encounter—whether it is the chiming of your cell phone, the knock at your door, or the beginning of a committee meeting. You can also do it through simple acts of generosity and kindness, such as letting another go first in the checkout line, picking up a dropped parcel for someone, or smiling at a stranger. More concretely, you can bless those persons outside your circle of friendships by calling your government representative about a piece of legislation and expressing your opinion clearly but kindly; taking a moment to say hello and affirming by your personal acknowledgment the holiness of a homeless person as you drop a coin in his or her can; making yourself available to help a harried father or mother at the grocery store; working cheerfully on a Habitat for Humanity project; praying for each person who comes into your house of worship; or finding a common cause with someone whose political views differ from your own.

Staying alert to opportunities for blessing others in every encounter opens our hearts to larger ways we can bless the world through financial generosity, political involvement, and caring service.

DAY 16

You Are a Channel of Divine Abundance

[Jesus said,] "I have come that you might have life in all its abundance."

—John 10:10, AP

We live in a world grounded in and permeated by divine abundance. Divine energy and inspiration flow through our every cell and every thought. The omniactive and omnipresent God still speaks throughout our world, luring us forward to new and surprising personal and planetary adventures in abundant living.

Sadly, though we live in a world characterized by divine abundance, many of us still see the world in terms of scarcity and isolation. All too often we perceive ourselves as lacking sufficient energy, insight, intelligence, talent, and money to experience personal fulfillment and really make a difference in the lives of others. What causes this scarcity mentality? I believe it results from viewing ourselves as independent and isolated, whether as a person, as a nation, or as a religious community. In Christian theology, another word for this isolated individualism is alienation. By contrast, living in terms of abundance is the result of perceiving our connectedness to God, loved ones, and the wider community, regardless of inner or outer conditions of poverty or wealth.

Faith awakens us to a deeper reality of God's lively and energetic presence in our lives through relationships that sustain and empower us. Faith in God as our loving companion enables us to risk giving to others generously, knowing that God will always supply our deepest needs. God's wellspring of insight and energy constantly replenishes our lives, especially when we awaken to the abundance that is our birthright.

Two of the most important questions put to mainstream and progressive Christians today are "How much do you expect of God?" and "How much do you expect of yourself?" I believe that God wants us to be bold—to expect great things from God and ourselves in our prayers and actions. Divine energy abounds, constantly inspiring, guiding, enlightening, and energizing us. God's energy is infinite! The main reason we do not access it is because we do not expect it or seek it. I am not talking about expecting supernatural miracles or violations of the basic laws of nature but simply opening ourselves to God's lively presence in every event. What does it mean to say that the energy that birthed the universe is birthing each moment of your experience? What would it be like for you to believe that, though you are finite in experience and power, nevertheless you are connected with the infinite Life of the universe? In a lively, relational, God-inspired universe, "nature" is much more surprising, energetic, and transformative than even quantum physicists can imagine. Accordingly, we can expect more of God and ourselves than we typically do. When we doubt our ability to be God's partners in transforming the world, we are called to remember that the power of Jesus the Healer and Teacher is being given to us moment by moment so that we might do "greater" works than he in embodying his ministry of healing and abundant life today.

John 2:1-11 describes Jesus transforming more than one hundred gallons of water into an equal amount of wine. Whether we understand this event as a sign of divine power, a metaphor for the new creation in Jesus' ministry, or a transformational acceleration of natural processes through spiritual practices, this event portrays the celebratory reality of divine abundance in our lives.

God delights in celebration! God's most creative work in the world and your life is still ahead of you. Like the stewards who carried water to Jesus, you can be a partner in God's abundant celebration of life. God is counting on your participation just as God counted on the efforts of the wine steward and the young boy who shared his lunch. Without them—and without you—God's abundance will not be fully released into the world.

God's energy is constantly flowing within all of our lives. By allowing ourselves to be generous channels of this abundant flow, we experience the fullness of God's presence and share that lively presence with others. This is the "practical mysticism" that enables us to experience God's abundant life at the very same time we share our lives with others. Indeed, as we share more, we discover that we have more—indeed, much more—of what is truly important in life. Living in God's abundance, we find that there is always more to share and enjoy and celebrate.

A Prayer for the Adventure

Abundantly creative God, inspire us to live by your abundance. Inspire us to believe more, to trust more, to love more, and to share more. Let us bring our gifts to you, like the stewards at that wedding feast, that together we may transform the mundane into the marvelous. Help us delight in loaves abounding and wine flowing for all your children. Amen.

CHOOSING YOUR OWN AFFIRMATION

God's abundant inspiration and energy constantly flow in and through us. Every cell and encounter is energized by God's presence. But we cut off the flow of God's life-transforming presence by our inattentiveness and lack of imagination. Affirmations help us pay attention to our role as partners in sharing God's abundant life and love with all whom we meet. Try repeating one or more of the following affirmations today:

- God's abundance flows through my life toward others.
- I share God's abundance with everyone I meet.
- I expect great things from God in (*a particular situation*).
- With God's help, I expect great things from myself in (*a particular situation*).

YOUR HOLY IMAGINATION

In today's imaginative prayer, I invite you to envision yourself as a guest at the wedding feast at Cana. Take time to read John 2:1-10, slowly meditating on its meaning for your life today.

Visualize yourself at a joyous wedding celebration. You are rejoicing in the love of two friends who have chosen to make a lifetime commitment. Where is the celebration taking place? Who is in attendance? Are you accompanied by a companion? What are you eating and drinking? Take time to experience the scene of the wedding celebration.

Because you are a close friend of the couple, you have been given responsibility for supervising the wedding celebration. Midway through the celebration, the caterer comes to you in distress. Someone has left more than half of the wine at the catering office. They will not be able to replenish the wine for over an hour. When you hear this news, how do you feel? What goes through your mind?

You remember that Jesus the Healer is among the wedding guests. What do you say to him? After a few minutes of conversation, Jesus asks you to fill the empty wine bottles with water. How do you initially respond to his request?

Eventually you recruit a few friends to help fill the bottles, and then Jesus prays over them. He then asks you to taste the contents. How does it taste? (Suspend your rational judgment for a moment.) What kind of wine does Jesus bring forth? How do you feel after experiencing this transformation?

As you look at your life, where are you feeling depleted? What areas do you need to open to God's lively and abundant energy? Take a moment and open to let God's abundant power flow in and through your life. What is it like to feel connected to divine power? Do you feel refreshed, renewed, joyful, and free? Experience God's power flowing from you to support the lives of those around you. How does it feel to be a channel of blessing and nurture to others?

Conclude by giving thanks for God's abundant power that flows into your life and from your life to others. Thank God for the gift of partnership that brings forth wonders when we least expect them.

LIVING ADVENTUROUSLY

Our scarcity thinking and acting often impede the flow of divine generosity in our lives. While providing for the survival, comfort, and long-term security of your family is important, sharing your material gifts, energy, and time generously with others is equally important. Looking at your life today, where do you sense God calling you to faithful generosity? What might be the cost of that generosity? Where are you blocking the flow of divine abundance? What joyous surprises might occur if you committed yourself to abundant living and abundant sharing?

> What joyous surprises might occur if you committed yourself to abundant living and abundant sharing?

In everyday life, this might mean moving toward a personal tithe, that is, 10 percent of your income, to your community of faith and other benevolences. It might also mean making a special financial gift, over and above your pledge or tithe, in response to a recent natural disaster. It could mean devoting time to tutoring a child, supporting a single parent, volunteering at a soup kitchen or a home for battered persons, or helping build or renovate a house in an area where adequate housing is needed. In my experience, the time and money we share with others creates a spiritual connectedness that enriches our lives in ways we cannot fully imagine.

DAY 17

We Give and Receive God's Love

Strive for God's reign and its righteousness and all these things will be given to you as well.

—Matthew 6:33, AP

The story of the woman with the alabaster jar (Matt. 26:6-13; Mark 14:3-9; John 12:1-8) has been celebrated in myth and legend throughout Christian history and has gained new popularity with Dan Brown's fictional mystery *The Da Vinci Code*. Mary's identity and relationship with Jesus are shrouded in mystery.[2] Some suggest she was one of Jesus' leading disciples, while others imagine that she might have been Jesus' wife. While such speculations probably will never be fully verified, the story of the woman who anointed Jesus points to the dynamic interplay of giving and receiving in the spiritual adventure. Breaking through the barriers of gender and social propriety, she lavishly and extravagantly anointed Jesus' head and feet. Mutuality is not just a matter of our personal relationships; it relates to the whole of life. It calls us to embody our theology in the practices of daily living by immersing ourselves in the deep relatedness that joins God and humankind in every encounter.

Despite their unique portrayals of the woman who anointed Jesus, the Gospel narratives affirm the woman's radical generosity and Jesus' equally radical receptivity. The onlookers were angry and aghast at the woman's anointing of Jesus with the finest perfume. They protested that the money could have been given to the poor. Indeed, their anger is well-founded—in a linear, individualistic, closed-system universe. Their zero-sum thinking accurately reflected their vision of a limited universe in which we never have enough resources for our daily needs and in which your gain is my loss. But that's not the world in which Jesus ministered and lived. Jesus saw himself constantly connected to an infinite source of abundant life-energy.

Jesus did not abandon the poor, but he also recognized that without love, beauty, and healthy relationships, economic well-being is of little worth. Indeed, persons of modest means may know more than the wealthy about love, simple beauty, and healthy interdependent relatedness. He also knew, as we know today, that there are truly enough of the earth's resources for all humankind—if we commit ourselves to simplicity, generosity, and creativity.

The woman with the alabaster jar saw the universe and her own personal life in terms of divine abundance. While her gift diminished her savings, it added beauty and stature to her life, for she knew that she was connected to a wellspring of divine energy that can never be depleted.

This encounter demonstrates the essential interdependence of life in which our lives emerge from countless factors and, by their very existence, add something important to the world around us. We are all part of the intricately connected "body of Christ" that embraces our faith communities and the planet. While pain and abuse may at times characterize our relationships, the deeper spiritual reality of relatedness, grounded in God's own intimate but universal giving and receiving, is one of support, care, and sustenance. When she anointed Jesus, this woman was simply letting God's abundant and loving energy flow through her, replenishing her own life as she nourished Jesus. She was preparing him for his eventual death, but just as importantly, she was also nurturing and celebrating his life and her love for him in that holy and spacious moment.

In the dynamic ecology of life, giving and receiving are part of a cosmic dance that is lived out, consciously or unconsciously, in every moment of our lives. Just as the woman gave generously from her heart, Jesus enabled her to be a giver by his willing receptivity. Jesus welcomed her into his life and let her touch him with love and intimacy, even though social and religious customs frowned on intimate encounters between men and women outside their immediate family. I believe that God also welcomes our gifts of loving generosity. God wants to be the receiver as well as the giver of life's beauty and blessings.

In truth, there are no absolute ethical or theological distinctions between those who are givers and receivers, and no one is excluded from the dynamic interplay of giving and receiving. We all are partners in the interrelatedness of all creation. Those who give today may be vulnerable tomorrow, and in desperate need of loving touch and gentle care. This is the ultimate foundation of Christian generosity. There is no ultimate boundary between "us" and "them" or "rich" and "poor," though our material and economic status may differ radically. When we volunteer at a soup kitchen or shelter, visit a nursing home, or tutor in an after-school program, our spiritual growth is intimately related to the receptivity of those whom we serve. Those we serve allow us to grow in spirit and generosity by their willingness to let us serve them. When we fail to recognize that our giving is dependent on their open arms, our actions will diminish their sense of value and worthiness.

Graceful as the journey is, we must never rest in our commitment to be God's shalom partners. We are called to work for universal health care, affordable housing, full employment, and quality education for all persons because "we are all in this together" in the energetic interdependence of life. Whether we describe this interdependence in terms of the lively body of Christ or the global spiritual and moral ecology, our giving and receiving reflect God's omniactive generosity that seeks the flourishing of all things.

We grow in spirit when we let the "poor" give to us out their apparent material scarcity, *and* when we share our abundance not out of our superiority to the poor and vulnerable but in recognition of our common humanity. God's bounty flows through our lives to others and returns to us in unexpected ways and from unexpected sources when we awaken to the essential interdependence of life.

A Prayer for the Adventure

Abundant and Living God, we open our hands to receive your blessings as we share your blessings with others. We open our hands to receive from those to whom we give. Bless our gifts and inspire us to holy receptivity as we live each day by your abundant grace. Amen.

Choosing Your Own Affirmation

In the individualistic ethos of American life, we are tempted to think we can go it alone, only to discover that our lives depend on the commitments and care of people we never meet. Our lives also touch others in ways that are life-transforming, even though we may not know it at the time. In the midst of this often overlooked reality, spiritual affirmations remind us of the holy interrelatedness that makes each of our encounters sacred.

- I give and receive God's love in every encounter.
- I am constantly giving and receiving grace and love throughout the day.
- I give and receive God's love in (*a specific encounter*).
- I receive God's love in (*a specific encounter*).

Your Holy Imagination

Take time to read Matthew 26:6-13 meditatively, letting the words soak in and take root in your life. Today you will experience the scripture from Jesus' point of view. (You can, of course, turn the story around and play the role of the woman as well, since the imagination is not confined by gender, sexual orientation, or religious title.)

It has been a long day, and you are tired from the interplay of travel, work, and the company of your associates. As the day ends, you have one more social event. You've been invited to dinner by a close business associate and friend. Take a moment to ponder who, among your friends, has invited you to dinner. As you arrive at the home, you are welcomed by your host and her or his family. What does their home look like? Other persons are also invited. Do you recognize any of them? The smell of good food permeates the air. What do you smell? What foods do you imagine will be served for dinner?

As you settle down for conversation, you notice a stranger coming toward you. Though that person looks familiar, you do not really know him or her. The person sits beside you and asks if you would like a foot massage. How do you respond? Do you accept or decline the offer? (If you decline, take a moment to imagine what you will say and how the other person will respond. Ponder what you might have missed as you continue on with dinner and drinks.)

If you accept the offer, let yourself imagine the following adventure. See the stranger humbly taking off your shoes and socks and beginning to massage your feet. How does it feel to receive that intimate hospitality from a stranger? He or she takes out some fragrant massage oil and begins massaging the oil into your feet and between your toes. Experience the feeling of touch and the fragrant scent of oil. As he or she finishes gently anointing your feet, hear the stranger say the following words: "Thank you for letting me serve you this evening." How does hearing these words make you feel? Are you surprised? What do you say in return?

Conclude this meditation, if you wish, by visualizing the rest of the evening to come—the drinks, the dinner, the conversation, and the sense of warmth and nurture you carry with you from the gift of the unexpected massage—with a sense of gratitude for the holy interdependence of life.

LIVING ADVENTUROUSLY

Today, take time to live out your affirmations in the many encounters you will have throughout the day. Be mindful of the interplay of giving and receiving. Notice how you respond to the hospitality and giving of others. (Are you receptive? Do you feel awkward?) Note the opportunities you have to nurture another's life in your interactions. If you have the opportunity to help others in need, examine your response to them. If you are able, do or say something that honors their life experience.

If you regularly volunteer in programs that serve persons in need, explore your attitudes toward those you serve. Do your relationships nurture their sense of value and self-esteem? Do they support their creativity and freedom? Are you thankful for the opportunity to serve? Remember the gift they are giving you by providing you with an occasion to be part of the lively relatedness of God's love.

DAY 18

We Can Experience God
in the Least of These

Just as you did it to one of the least of these who are members of my family, you did it to me.

—Matthew 25:40

This week we are reflecting on the centrality of holy relationships in our lives as Christians. Christian compassion is grounded in the vision of divine-human partnership that radiates across the universe, shaping cells and cities, congregations and countries. What does it mean to affirm that we live in a sea of relatedness in which every act touches countless others, directly and indirectly?

This sea of relatedness allows physicists to affirm the reality of "nonlocal" causation. According to quantum physics, the energy of our lives, manifested in thoughts, feelings, and actions, shapes the lives of other beings, even though we have no direct contact with them or awareness of them. In light of this theory, as we ponder the power of prayer to shape the world, we can visualize our prayers creating a positive "field of force" around those for whom we pray, enabling them to be more attentive to God's dream for their lives and opening the door for more lively expressions of divine love and relatedness in the world. As a nonlocal causal phenomenon, prayer touches others immediately without the need of any form of physical contact. In many ways, all prayer is "distant healing" prayer. Our prayerful intentions for the highest and best of another also enable God to transform that person's world in new and creative ways.

The words of Matthew 25:31-46 inspire us to personal generosity and social action. In this passage, Jesus speaks of judgment in terms of our recognition of our lives for what they really are in terms of our values, personal commitments, and relationships. The righteous ones are surprised at

Jesus' revelation of his presence in their everyday lives: "For I was hungry and you gave me food, I was thirsty and you gave me something to drink, I was a stranger and you welcomed me, I was naked and you gave me clothing, I was sick and you took care of me, I was in prison and you visited me" (vv. 35-36). With them, we must also ask as we go about our daily lives, "When did we see you, feed you, clothe you, or visit you?" (vv. 37-39, AP).

This passage invites us to live a theology of extraordinary interdependence in the midst of ordinary life. In actuality, what we consider ordinary life is the window through which we can regularly behold the presence of God, who seeks healing and wholeness in every encounter and every person. If we look beneath the surface, we will see the face of God in every face and touch the body of Christ in every caress.

It is important to recognize that something more is at work in this passage than simply our awareness of God's presence in those we encounter. This passage is also a striking portrayal of divine receptivity. Could it be that Jesus really means, "As you did it to one of the least of these who are members of my family, you did it to me"?

Do our actions really contribute something of value to God's own experience? While it is easy to think of our political and social actions shaping our fellow creatures, it is more challenging to consider the impact of our actions on the quality of God's life! If God is omniscient and experiences all things, then everything we do makes a difference to God. Our thoughts and actions shape God's experience and affect God's future actions. What would your life look like if you truly believed that God is a different God because we have chosen certain actions and priorities rather than others?

God is not merely a judge who objectively evaluates our lives from a distance. God feels our lives from inside and receives our experience into God's own life. Christian ethics asks, "How will my actions shape my neighbor's life and bring justice and shalom to the world?" It also asks, "How will my actions shape God's experience? Will my actions give God a more beautiful or an uglier world?"

I believe that this is the deeper meaning of Matthew 25:31-46. In the interdependence of life, each act is as deeply felt by God as well as by our neighbor. We are called to contribute beauty, creativity, goodness, and compassion to God's evolving experience of the world.

A Prayer for the Adventure

God, whose heart beats in all hearts, who hears our prayers, delights in our joy, celebrates our achievements, and mourns our losses, may we truly give our lives to you. May we do something beautiful for you, and may we delight in giving you delight at the evolving joy of all creation. Amen.

CHOOSING YOUR OWN AFFIRMATION

Our ability to sense God's presence in our lives is a matter of spiritual awareness and practice. While it is normal to doubt the divine impact of our actions or overlook the presence of God in the ins and outs of our daily living, affirmations illumine our lives and help us to act on our commitment to contribute something of beauty to God and our neighbor.

- I see God in "the least of these."
- I see God in (*a particular person*).
- I do something beautiful for God in every situation.
- I do something beautiful for God in (*a particular situation*).

YOUR HOLY IMAGINATION

Gently and meditatively read Matthew 25:31-46, reflecting on what it means to see and serve God in "the least of these." Take time to be still. Who are "the least of these" in your experience right now? Who lacks livelihood, self-esteem, human companionship, or basic health and human services? Who is most vulnerable?

Visualize some faces of "the least of these" in your life. Empathize with their pain and alienation, the sense of hopelessness. Then take time to look deeper. See the face of Christ blending with their faces. How does this change your perspective on these persons? How does it change your perception of God's presence in their lives and yours?

Look deeper at your own life with its pain and challenges. See the face of Christ blending with your own face. In your imagination, visualize yourself greeting one of the least of these and sharing with them a gift that will enable them to experience God's abundant life. Experience the Christ in you greeting the Christ in them.

Conclude with gratitude for your new insights and the opportunity to see Christ in all persons.

LIVING ADVENTUROUSLY

Our spiritual insights are intended to be practiced in the midst of everyday life. While ultimately all of us are both blessed and vulnerable, today we are challenged to respond to the most obviously vulnerable persons we encounter in everyday life or even through the media.

Knowing that divine generosity is constantly flowing through your life toward others, consider taking time today to be more aware of vulnerable persons in your community. While you are committed to be aware of God's presence in unexpected places, you are also challenged to practice your faith with intentional acts of extravagant generosity. You may, for example, join or organize a local chapter of a group such as Bread for the World in order to influence legislation related to issues of hunger and poverty. You may choose to volunteer at a center for families who have experienced domestic violence. Your faith community may want to support an after-school program for at-risk children or unwed teenage mothers. After appropriate training in issues of bereavement and loss, you may choose to volunteer at your local hospice or initiate a bereavement group in your congregation. If you drink coffee, you may choose to purchase fair-trade coffee to ensure that persons in developing countries receive higher wages and more humane working conditions. In all these situations, may your goal be to do something beautiful for God and to discover Christ's presence in life's most distressing situations.

DAY 19

God Is Present in the Lives
of Our Enemies

*Love your enemies and pray for those who persecute you, so that you
may be children of your Father in heaven.*

—Matthew 5:44-45

Taking seriously the doctrines of omnipresence and omniactivity
will transform your life. One of the hardest theological facts to put
into practice is the insight that if God is present and active everywhere,
then God is present in your enemies as well as your loved ones. Many of
us were raised with an implicit Calvinist theology, which describes divine
power and knowledge in terms of predestination. From this perspective,
God foreordains some to salvation and others to damnation. Those who are
predestined to damnation fall outside the circle of divine and, accordingly,
our human love and ethical consideration. Others of us were raised to see
salvation dualistically in terms of unbridgeable chasms between saved and
unsaved, and heaven and hell. While many of us have intellectually
rejected these dualistic doctrines, we may still polarize the world's population in terms of doers of good and evil. We may project our own personal
or national "shadow" side on other persons and nations, feeling that they
can do no good, while we and our country can do no evil!

In contrast, I believe that in a world of creativity and freedom, God
constantly and unambiguously seeks wholeness in every situation and for
every person. To be sure, the impact of the interplay of environment, genetics, and personal choice can limit and obscure the experience of God in our
lives and the lives of others. Despite God's passion for beauty and shalom
for all creation, some persons consistently choose violence, self-interest,
and destruction. Still, even these persons are not fully responsible for their
harmful decisions. For instance, we know that sexual predators often expe-

rienced sexual abuse as children; violent criminals and physical abusers often come from abusive and alienating environments. Narcissistic adults are often the children of parents who denied the child's unique feelings, needs, and subjective experience. The "sins of the parents" become especially tragic when narcissistically and physically abused children become national or business leaders.

We can see the tragic personal and global impact of destructive parenting and decision making in the lives of such tyrants as Adolf Hitler and Saddam Hussein. Yet, despite their political violence megalomania, God was still working in their lives. Although God's still, small voice was barely audible in their lives, God continued to call them constantly to repentance, transformation, and new life.

Sadly, the profound influence of the past, whether personal choices, genetics, family of origin, or social environment, is often so great that God's vision for our concrete experience may simply be preventative rather than creative. In a particular situation, we may have turned so far from God's ideal for our lives that the greatest good may simply be the prevention of further violence, alienation, and destruction. As the philosopher Alfred North Whitehead notes, God's aim for beauty and complexity of experience may sometimes have to be "the best for that impasse."[3] In particularly harmful situations, God may seek simply to minimize the violence, pain, and indignity that is perpetrated upon innocent victims as the first step to the possible transformation of a person's life. God does not coerce "evildoers" but seeks to save them by moving within their lives and the lives of persons who may help them experience an alternative way of life. Still, we can respond to life's traumas, the challenges of our environment and family of origin, and personal decisions in ways that reflect God's vision of healing and new life.

At times, our own anger and self-preoccupation also cloud our experience of God's vision for our lives. But still God is working within our own personal conflicts and tendencies toward polarizing words or behavior. When we encounter violence and injustice, God may inspire us not only to love the "evildoer" but also to restrain future evil through protection, confrontation, and political involvement.

Jesus recognized the interplay of tragedy and grace within the interplay of divine creativity and human freedom when he asserted that God makes the sun to rise on the righteous and the unrighteous alike (Matt. 5:45). Outsiders, prison inmates, prostitutes, and tax collectors are God's beloved children, along with law-abiding, morally upright, and socially responsible citizens. The light of God shines in and on our enemies as well as on those we love.

"Lived omnipresence," grounded in our recognition of the ubiquitous light and love of God, is our only hope to escape the polarization and culture wars that characterize our current political and cultural environment. Seeing the hidden holiness in your enemy or opponent does not lead to political or interpersonal passivity. It may lead to greater political and personal involvement on behalf of the most vulnerable members of our world community. When we see the light of God within ourselves and others, we cultivate a holy self-affirmation that embraces the other as God's beloved child, despite our differences. Grounded in the vision of God's presence in every person, we can challenge injustice at national, domestic, and interpersonal levels while, nevertheless, treating those with whom we must contend with reverence and prayerful respect. This was the path of Jesus and also the way of Mahatma Gandhi, Martin Luther King Jr., and Desmond Tutu.

A Prayer for the Adventure

God, whose love embraces all things, awaken us to your love for those whom we call enemies. Give us wisdom to protect our highest interests and the highest interests of our homeland, while seeing your presence in those who challenge and threaten us, and those who love their own homelands. Let us work for justice and peace and reconciliation, trusting your love when our love reaches its limits. In partnership with your all-embracing love, let us bring shalom to this good earth. In Christ's name. Amen.

Choosing Your Own Affirmation

Transforming our vision of our enemies is the result of constant self-awareness, because the natural tendency is to demonize our personal and political opponents. In that spirit, I invite you to entertain the following affirmations today.

- God loves my enemies as well as me.
- I experience God's presence in (*a difficult person*).
- I experience God's presence in a (*difficult international political figure*).

Your Holy Imagination

In today's imaginative prayer, first meditate quietly on Matthew 5:45. Reflect on the difficult persons in your life. While not excusing their behavior, look deeper into their lives. See their deepest identity in Christ. Pray that they will discover their own identity as God's beloved children and live out God's dream for them.

Visualize a national or international figure that you strongly dislike. Experience fully your attitude toward that person. While not excusing the individual's behavior or supporting his or her policies, see yourself letting go of that negative attitude. Instead, see this person's deepest identity in Christ. Pray that this figure more fully discovers her or his identity as God's beloved child and follows the path of justice.

Living Adventurously

Practice spiritual mindfulness today. Reflect on the quality of your thought and speech patterns. Do you subtly or explicitly dismiss or demonize certain persons? How do your attitudes toward them shape your language and behavior toward them? Make a commitment to gently and prayerfully transform your language, attitudes, and behavior. When you contend with such persons or seek redress for injustices committed toward others or yourself, make a commitment to treat them with heartfelt respect and reverence as well as assertiveness. This is what it means to speak the truth in love.

Spiritual maturity also involves distancing ourselves from the polarization of political factions and the media. Watching television prayerfully can be a contemporary spiritual discipline. When you begin to feel increasingly angry toward or alienated from a national political figure, social group, ethnic minority, or international figure, pause for a moment simply to breathe mindfully and reflect on why you are so angry or polarized. You may have to turn off the television in order to recover your spiritual center. Does your anger help the process of bringing peace and justice into the world? How might you transform your anger into action on behalf of the oppressed, marginalized, and vulnerable?

DAY 20

God Calls Me to Live by Forgiveness

Peter came to Jesus and asked, "Lord, how many times shall I forgive my brother when he sins against me? Up to seven times?" Jesus answered, "I tell you, not seven times, but seventy-seven times."
—Matthew 18:21-22, NIV

Jesus was once asked how often we should forgive a person who has hurt us. His listeners probably expected him to place a limit on forgiveness. Instead, he stated the symbolic number of "seventy-seven times," or infinite forgiveness, as the appropriate limit for our response to others' imperfections.

It is important to recognize that forgiveness is a metaphysical as well as a personal virtue. Each moment of our lives involves forgiveness; forgiveness is essentially birthing and dying—coming into being and then letting go in order to grasp the next moment in its immediacy. Each new experience requires going beyond the impact of the previous moment, "forgiving it," and placing it in the past. Although we cannot hold on to the past in its immediacy, we can choose to bring the past into our present experience in ways that bring either joy or unhappiness. Past failures can keep us from pursuing future adventures; they can also teach us how to pursue them with greater wisdom. Depending on the presence of forgiveness, painful encounters can stand in the way of exploring new relational or professional possibilities, or they can launch us into new careers or vocations.

Forgiveness is based on the ability to transform the meaning of the past in our lives today. God does not place painful events in our lives to build our character or test our faith, but God does work within negative circumstances to open our hearts and deepen our awareness of the brokenness in the world, and to claim our vocation as God's healing partners.

Forgiving is not forgetting but transforming the meaning of the past in the present moment. Today, medical researchers talk about the "forgiveness factor." Medical studies have shown that persons who let go of negative events experience a greater sense of well-being than those who continue to hold grudges because of past injustices. In authentic forgiveness, the past event is not forgotten but experienced as an opportunity for greater freedom, love, and creativity. This does not mean that we minimize its impact. In order to claim wholeness of body, mind, and spirit, we must always remember our own or others' negative experiences, such as sexual abuse, holocaust, slavery, narcissistic abuse, unfair labor practices, or exclusion, and we must commit ourselves to preventing them from recurring. We are called also to choose an attitude that affirms God's light and love, as well as beauty and truth in the midst of our remembrance and advocacy.

As a spiritual discipline, forgiveness is a gentle process. It cannot be hurried. To find wholeness, we must fully experience our anger, hatred, depression, and despair about life's traumatic experiences. We may benefit from the wise and creative partnership of a spiritual guide, pastoral counselor, psychotherapist, or psychiatrist as we seek to respond creatively to our pain. We may even need medication in addition to meditation, or "prayer and Prozac," as my colleague Dale Matthews, MD, suggests. A healthy theology of forgiveness must not short-circuit the healing process with superficial platitudes or simplistic advice. While we may begin the process of forgiveness intellectually and spiritually, we must experience the psychological and physical alignment of our bodies, emotions, and memories with our intention of forgiveness. Alignment of our relationships must come next in order for healing to take place. Jesus' words on the cross, "Father, forgive them, for they do not know what they are doing" (Luke 23:34), inspire us to let go of the painful past. They also challenge us to remember the tragic impact of sufferings of many individuals from personal and social evil. The reality is that abuse and violence are often passed down from generation to generation and are supported by unjust social and political systems.[4] Only God's power of forgiving love can transform them.

Forgiveness must be balanced by social activism and interpersonal assertiveness that seeks to minimize suffering and injustice and to call persons and institutions to live out God's vision of shalom. To quote some words I saw inscribed on a bench at Kirkridge Retreat Center, we are challenged to both "picket and pray." We are to actively oppose violence and abuse in any form—whether interpersonal, institutional, or political—but also to pray for the transformation of our own hearts and of oppressive systems and abusive persons in our lives. Our hope for forgiveness is grounded in the faith that we and others can experience transforming love even in the midst of confrontation. However, the call to confront, especially when it comes to persons who have deeply hurt us, must come in the context of our feeling strong and safe. Especially in situations of abuse, no confrontation should take place without much prayerful preparation and the guidance of a psychotherapist or other professional.

In the end, forgiveness is a form of divine healing. As we embrace divine forgiveness in our lives, our memories and our actions—our lives—are transformed and made whole. To forgive is not only to affirm our value as God's beloved children but also to recognize that same holiness in those whose actions temporarily disguise God's presence. While we will not allow ourselves or others to be abused or treated unjustly, we also look for signs of healing in the most unlikely of places as we work for the healing of ourselves, our families, and the earth.

A Prayer for the Adventure

Holy One, who is completely open to our joy and pain, you know our hearts and intentions. You know where we have missed the mark, chosen evil over good, and comfort over justice. You know where we have hurt others as well as ourselves. We confess our alienation and brokenness and ask that your forgiving love give us a new start. Show us where we have gone astray, and give us the courage and insight to begin again and again and again. In the name of the Healer Jesus. Amen.

Choosing Your Own Affirmation

I invite you to contemplate the reality that forgiveness is a choice as well as a grace. Our intention to live by forgiveness liberates us to see the world with new eyes. We learn to let go of our imperfection as we commit ourselves to spiritual growth. Forgiveness frees us to become God's partners in transforming the world in new and amazing ways.

- I forgive myself and claim God's love for me.
- By God's forgiveness, I am freed from past pain and injustice.
- I claim God's forgiveness of myself and others.
- God is with me as I seek to forgive (*a particular person*).

Your Holy Imagination

Do not attempt the following exercise if you are still deeply struggling with the impact of abuse, sexism, racism, and injustice; you may not have the interpersonal support to forgive in such situations. If you are struggling with issues of forgiveness without an adequate support community, take time today just to rest and relax in God's light and love. Forgiveness is a communal as well as a personal issue. Accordingly, it is important to have personal, spiritual, and professional companions with you on your pathway to forgiveness.

In this healing exercise, take a moment to bathe yourself in God's care. With every breath, imagine divine energy entering your life and surrounding you with a protective shield. Whatever has happened in the past, know that in this moment you are now protected and surrounded by God's loving care.

Take a moment to recall and feel your emotions about a personal slight. (It is often good to begin with something modest. If you want to tackle a more significant experience of pain or abuse, you may choose to do this exercise with an experienced spiritual friend.) Imagine the scene. What happened? What actions or words hurt you? How did you feel at the time? What are your feelings about the event today? How do you feel about the person who caused you this pain?

Now, visualize Jesus as your companion in that situation. Experience his love and care for you. Tell Jesus about how you felt at the time and how you feel now. How does Jesus respond to you? What words does he say or what action does he take? Feel Jesus' nearness. Perhaps he hugs you or stands between you and the one who has hurt you.

If possible, even as Jesus companions and protects you, sense Jesus' compassion for the one who has hurt you. Can you view that person as a beloved but misguided child of God? You may experience Jesus breaking the chain of pain and injustice so that both of you can experience new freedom. (If this part of the exercise is too painful, skip this section and simply focus on Jesus' comfort and care for you. That will be enough to support your healing process.)

Conclude this exercise with a sense of God's presence protecting and guiding you. Know that you are ultimately safe in God's care and that God is healing your life right now. Give thanks for God's loving presence now and in the future.[5]

LIVING ADVENTUROUSLY

In the spirit of the last exercise, your participation in this practice should arise from your sense of safety and growing forgiveness. If you find yourself feeling unsafe, emotionally fragile, or at risk, please seek spiritual and professional guidance that will enable you to experience the fullness of God's presence in your past or present painful memories and encounters.

Now, if you feel that it is safe to do so, take a moment to consider persons from whom you feel estranged. Imagine their faces and the burdens they bear. If you are able to forgive them, perform a ritual to symbolize your new freedom. For example, you may draw the scene of the event, place a circle around it to represent God's light and love, and then carefully burn the picture or tear it up and flush it down the toilet as a symbol of letting go. You may also find it in yourself to pray for greater forgiveness and for the true well-being of one who has hurt you. If it is appropriate and you are at peace in your forgiveness, you may choose to communicate your forgiveness to the other in writing or speech, while at the same time letting go of your need to have any particular response on her or his part. Forgiveness is as much about your need to experience peace and reconciliation within yourself as it is about the other's acceptance of your forgiveness.

Again, do not hurry or force your forgiveness processes. Honor where you are on our journey and have modest expectations of yourself. At all times, deal gently with yourself along your journey to wholeness and healing.

DAY 21

God Wants Us to Love Ourselves as Well as Our Neighbors

Love your neighbor as you love yourself.

—Mark 12:31, NCV

For the last several years, I have facilitated colleague support and spiritual formation groups for pastors at various stages of their careers—beginning, middle, and preretirement. I have found that one of the greatest challenges of pastoral ministry is healthy self-care and self-affirmation. Often pastors put everyone's needs ahead of themselves, their spouses or significant others, and family. Thinking themselves to be indispensable representatives of Christ, these pastors work tirelessly to minister to their congregations. They forget that God is always inspiring others within their congregations to be their partners in ministry. When pastors fail to take time to nurture their own spiritual and personal well-being, they often experience burnout, cynicism, illness, anger, and alienation. Their ministries suffer, and so do those around them!

Laypersons also have the same symptoms when they fail to care for their own well-being amid a lifetime of service to the church. Often laypersons feel guilty for taking time off from work and family responsibilities for spiritual renewal. Everyone needs sabbath time.[6] Like many pastors, they too fail to see the connection between healthy self-love and caring for others. What does it mean to love our neighbors as ourselves?

When Jesus asserted that we should love our neighbors as ourselves, he was expressing once again the profound theological truth that our love for ourselves and for others is intimately connected in the intricate ecology of life. We cannot wisely love others until we know how to love ourselves—and do it! In the dynamic and interdependent fabric of life, our wholeness and well-being and the wholeness and well-being of others are indivisible. Indeed, we cannot achieve our vocation in life apart from one another.

Alfred North Whitehead noted that authentic peace is the gift of an expansive vision in which our individual self-interest expands to include the well-being of others. In so doing, we reflect the divine passion for wholeness. God's passionate love for each unique moment of life always includes not only the well-being of our most immediate companions but also the whole earth. God wants our embrace of abundant life to bring joy and beauty to the lives of those around us. The key concept here is that God wants us to experience joy and wholeness as a means of enhancing the joy and health of others.

The practices of loving God, loving the world, loving our neighbor, and loving ourselves form an inseparable unity. We find God's presence not only in the natural world but also in the face of our neighbor and in our own personal adventures. If we affirm that "God is the circle whose center is everywhere and whose circumference is nowhere,"[7] then we will dedicate ourselves to helping each creature experience God's deep love for them. With Dorotheos of Gaza, we will recognize that loving God and others is interconnected as we all move from the circumference to the center of God's holy circle.

A Prayer for the Adventure

God, whose love centers on each creation and embraces all things, help me wake up to your loving embrace. Help me understand that I am your beloved child, fully encompassed by your care. Help me love myself through acts of self-acceptance and self-care. Let the love I feel from you flow to everyone I meet as I claim my role as your partner in mending the world. Amen.

CHOOSING YOUR OWN AFFIRMATION

Many of us see God everywhere except in our own lives. We affirm that grace abounds, but deep down we believe that we must be perfect in order to be loved and to love ourselves. Graceful affirmations transform our images of ourselves and others. As our minds are gently transformed, our bodies, emotions, and memories begin to reveal our growing experience of ourselves as God's beloved children, loving ourselves and loving each other.

- I love myself just as I am.
- I treat myself with love, taking time for rest and refreshment.
- My love for myself embraces everyone I meet.
- I love myself by (*a particular action*).
- I join my love for myself with my love for others by (*a particular action*).

YOUR HOLY IMAGINATION

In this imaginative prayer, live out the reality of Dorotheos's vision of the divine circle. According to Dorotheos, our spiritual growth can be visualized in terms of moving from the circumference to the center of God's circle of love: the closer we come to the divine center, the closer we come to one another; and the closer we come to one another, the closer we also come to God.

Begin your prayer time by breathing deeply into your belly. Feel your kinship with all things as you share in the holy breath of all creation.

Visualize your every breath filling you with energy and inspiration. Know that God is within you and all creation.

See yourself as part of a circle in which God is the center, radiating outward toward all things. Picture yourself on the circumference, surrounded by countless others. Take a moment simply to rejoice in the wonder of your life.

Now look more carefully at your companions around the circumference. Do you recognize anyone? Consider your deep connectedness. Think about their holiness as God's beloved children, whether they have two or four feet. Sense your lives flowing into one another in God's circle of love.

Next, picture yourself intentionally moving toward the center, where the omnipresent God can be experienced most fully. Notice that as you move toward the center, you become closer both physically and spiritually to your partners. Experience your growing unity and interdependence with all of life. See yourself giving and receiving love in your relationships with your companions. Take time to sense the divine creativity and love flowing through your life and the life of all things.

Conclude this imaginative prayer with thanksgiving for God's love, which joins and centers all things in healthy self-love and companionship.

LIVING ADVENTUROUSLY

Today's practice embodies your affirmations and imaginative prayer. As you reflect on your own life and its connectedness to all things within the divine community, where do you need to embody healthy love for yourself? What actions or practices affirm your life while contributing to the well-being of the universe and those around you?

As you look at the experiences of others, what small action can you take to support the well-being of another person in context of affirming your own personal wholeness? Make a commitment today to reach out lovingly toward one of your companions in ways that also bring joy and health to yourself.

WEEK
4

CALLED TO SERVICE

T he wisdom theology that permeates the Hebrew scriptures and the New Testament portrays the universe as lively, dynamic, and evolving. Scripture sees nature and history as a unified and interdependent whole. God's presence and activity permeate all things, human and nonhuman. Revelations burst forth from birds and trees, stars and mountains, unborn children and angelic hosts. Even the fabled narrative of Balaam's donkey suggests that the nonhuman world can be a medium of divine revelation to wayward humankind.[1]

Today, more than ever, we need to recover a unified and holistic vision of planetary and human life that is at the heart of the wisdom tradition of scripture. Although Christianity has often been guilty of confusing stewardship with dominion in its attitude toward nature, today a new vision of Christian faith, open to the insights of physics, biology, and ecology, brings healing to the modern rift between heaven and earth and humankind and the nonhuman world. While some Christians point our vision heavenward, believing that the meaning of this life is to be found in preparing for eternity, holistic and adventurous visions of faith affirm the eternal within the temporal, and the temporality of eternity. Today's spiritual adventurers live by the wisdom of Hildegard of Bingen, "Holy persons draw to themselves all that is earthly."[2]

Dynamic, holistic visions of life see humankind as a partner with God and the nonhuman world in our evolving planetary adventure. We are not alien to the natural world but creative and often destructive members of the planetary community. The universe is alive, and each creature has an immediate relationship with God. God guides each creature to its appropriate creativity. God also experiences every creature's quest to experience abundant life in its particular ecological and social context.

Today our calling is to assist God in healing the world, and this means the whole earth as well as humanity. Our responsibility as God's healing partners has never been greater, especially since we have been the major source of planetary and personal destruction. Our own spiritual evolution as well as our survival depends on how we respond to our many planetary crises. Our personal vocations cannot be separated from the reality of global warming and the ongoing extinction of animal species. We must fashion our spiritual lives in the context of massive homelessness following the Asian tsunami and Hurricane Katrina, the deaths of millions of children in Africa due to malnutrition and civil strife, and the reality of forty million Americans who cannot afford health insurance.

As we chart our own spiritual adventures, we must proclaim that we are creatures of both earth and heaven. If we are to be faithful to the One who affirmed "'Your will be done on earth as well as heaven," we must respond to the challenges of this world in light of our hopes for the life to come.

In the days ahead, we will explore our spiritual responsibilities in a lively, God-filled universe. Like Jesus, we are called as spirit persons to proclaim good news to all creation! As we deepen our earthly roots, we will experience our divine origins and destiny as God's partners in a dynamic and evolving planetary adventure. With the Catholic poet Gerard Manley Hopkins, we will delight in our experience of "God's grandeur" permeating all things. We will say yes to the earth and yes to the infinite future that lies ahead.

We Are Part of the Body of Christ

Now you are the body of Christ and individually members of it.
—1 Corinthians 12:27

Today, our image of the body of Christ embraces the planetary as well as human communities. To confine the body of Christ just to the Christian church would be to perpetuate an unhelpful dualism of sacred and secular, spirit and the world, humankind and nature, and Christian and non-Christian. While we may still identify Paul's understanding of particular spiritual gifts with the life of Christian congregations and the Christian community as a whole, we must recognize that our vocations call us to pursue healing of the earth as well as of humankind. The church as the body of Christ exists to join seamlessly the inner journey of contemplation and the outer journey of action in its vocation as God's partner in bringing healing and wholeness to all creation.

In these times we must image the body of Christ in terms of a holistic vision of divine-human community in which there is a continuum between body, mind, and spirit. Each part of the human body has a unique gift and function that arises from and contributes to its relationships with all the other parts of the body. Seen from a wider perspective, the body of Christ, like the church universal, the planet Earth, and the human body itself, is a temple of the Holy Spirit. From this perspective, we can imagine the mind of Christ permeating every cell and every soul, and consecrating each moment of life within that intricately connected whole that joins humankind and the planet.

Our personal vocation is to support the well-being of the planetary body of Christ as well as the church and the human community. This is the insight of Romans 8:18-28. Here Paul describes all creation as expectantly waiting for the fulfillment of humankind's spiritual vocation. What would your life look like if you really lived by the affirmation that your spiritual evolution can transform the planet? How would you live if you recognized that your well-being is intimately connected with the well-being of the complex and fragile ecology of life? Truly, adventurous, creation-affirming spirituality invites us to experience the unity of life in which our fate and the earth's fate are interconnected. Joining earth and heaven, our vocations are spiritual, communal, and planetary in nature.

A Prayer for the Adventure

Living Spirit in whom all things live, move, and have their being, we rejoice in the world you are creating. We rejoice in our bodies and in the body of Christ, which nurtures our lives in their entirety. Live through us, enlivening each cell. Love through us so that we may embrace the gifts of the whole earth and the congregation of which we are a part. Awaken us to our gifts for the whole as we receive the gifts of each part. In Christ's name. Amen.

CHOOSING YOUR OWN AFFIRMATION

It is clear that the survival of our planet requires the transformation of the human community. Our faith tradition tells us that we always have the opportunity to repent, that is, to turn around and to change our ways. We can more fully claim our place as stewards of the planet, whose vocation is to nurture and preserve the earth, through transforming our destructive ways of life. Affirmations remind us who we are and what we are called to be as stewards of life.

- I belong to the planetary body of Christ.
- My calling is to be God's partner in healing the world.
- I honor God's spirit in the nonhuman as well as human communities.
- My calling is to be God's partner in healing (*a part of our world*).
- I experience God's presence in (*a nonhuman creature*).

YOUR HOLY IMAGINATION

When our son was small, we gave him a blue-green stuffed pillow, covered with a map of the earth, called "Hug a Planet." He enjoyed playing catch with it, rolling it down the hall, and affectionately hugging his little planet Earth. Visualizing the earth in such a way helps us see the earth in all its wonder and fragility. Healing the earth involves the gifts of imagination, action, and affirmation, which enable us to cherish and preserve the good earth that gives us life.

Take a few moments simply to be still in gratitude for God's gift of life on this blue-green planet. Breathe gently, experiencing your relationship with all of life as you inhale and exhale. In your imagination, visualize the whole earth as one lively, interconnected community of human and non-human life forms. Visualize the dancing activity of these life forms, transcending the boundaries of nations, ethnic groups, and plant and animal species. Experience the earth as one great and awesome revelation of God, one great Life encompassing the many life forms, including your own life. Envision the cultures, climates, and energies of the earth flowing through you and nurturing you. From your particular place on the planet, imagine your many possible roles in healing the earth. What are you called to do to save the earth in your particular time and place? What is it like to experience your life as intimately related to everything else, bringing health and wholeness through your actions and commitments?

Conclude by thanking God for the wonder of this good earth and your unique place in it.

LIVING ADVENTUROUSLY

Rabbi Abraham Joshua Heschel proclaimed that "radical amazement" was the heart of the spiritual adventure. Today I invite you to commit yourself to experiencing the wonder of life in the nonhuman and human world in new and different ways. Recognize holiness in your animal companions. Watch documentaries about nondomestic creatures. Make a commitment to see every creature as a revelation of God.

As part of your stewardship, you may wish to support the nonhuman world through volunteering or contributing financially to groups whose goal is protecting the planet and its many species through political action or hands-on "re-creation" of damaged ecosystems. You may also wish to support a local chapter of the Humane Society or Animal Rescue as a way of easing the pain that domestic animals also experience.

DAY 23

Our Lives Can Heal the Body of Christ

If one member suffers, all suffer together with it; if one member is honored, all rejoice together with it.

—1 Corinthians 12:26

In the apostle Paul's vision of the body of Christ, every part is connected with and contributes to the health of the whole. In the body of Christ, no part is unnecessary or unimportant. Like the human body itself, the well-being of the humblest and smallest parts may be a matter of life and death for the organism as a whole. What appears obvious and attractive to the eye may be less important for survival than what is hidden and overlooked.

Paul's image of Christ's body suggests that we are cosmic as well as individual beings. We are not ultimately defined by our ethnicity, nation, or abilities but are connected first with the whole planet, and then with the whole universe. Our spirits are meant to embrace the planetary, solar, and galactic families as well as our immediate circle of friends and faith community. "Now you are the body of Christ and individually members of it" (1 Cor. 12:27).

Jewish and Christian spiritual formation involves discerning our vocation in community as well as in solitude. Our personal adventure embraces not only our human and nonhuman companions but our "cosmic" companions as well. Unity and diversity reflect the abundance of divine creativity that gives life to all things, human and nonhuman alike, on our planet and throughout the universe. Our gifts and choices are meant to support God's vision of wholeness and salvation not only for our earthly community but also for the solar system and beyond. The recent discovery of a double-helix nebula at the center of the Milky Way galaxy, eighty light-years, or about 470 trillion miles, long, reminds us that divine creativity and beauty are reflected both in the cosmos and in the microcosmic world of our own DNA and immune system.

Your existence is essential to the well-being of the body of Christ, but so are the existence of plankton, Amazon rain forests, and companion animals or pets and the swirling of galaxies and revolving of planets. Our calling is to find our place within the constantly evolving and interconnected universal body of Christ. In finding our authentic calling for this time and place, we support the vocational adventures of every other member of the body of Christ, here and throughout the universe. Radical amazement and wonder, reflected in commitment to healing and wholeness at the micro and macro levels, is the only appropriate response for those who seek to be God's partners in mending the world.

A Prayer for the Adventure

Healing hands of Jesus, touch our lives and touch our world. Move within every cell and every soul. Transform us that we might radiate your wholeness and healing as your companions in healing the world. Let healing abound; let every act and every word bring joy and wholeness to all creation. In the name of the Healer Jesus. Amen.

CHOOSING YOUR OWN AFFIRMATION

Commitment to spiritual transformation is an essential first step in exploring the cosmic, planetary, interpersonal, and corporate dimensions of the body of Christ. Living with both cosmic and personal spiritual affirmations awakens us to the relationship between our gifts and the healing of the cosmos and our own blue-green planet.

- I claim my vocation as God's partner in planetary healing.
- My gifts bring healing to my human and nonhuman companions.
- My gifts bring healing to (*a particular animal or human*).

YOUR HOLY IMAGINATION

In this meditation, I invite you to explore your unique gift within the cosmic body of Christ. After spending a few minutes in silent prayer, imagine yourself as part of a wondrous cosmic body that embraces the universe as we know it. Envisage this body's appearance and characteristics. Visualize the health and vitality of this glorious body—experience the whirling and spinning of galaxies, solar systems, and planets.

Now reflect on your vocation within this lively and beautiful body. What organ or cell are you within this cosmic body? What is your gift to the whole? In what ways are you contributing to the whole? In what ways do you need healing in order to fulfill your role? As you look at your place within the body, what parts of the body most nurture you? Can you identify these supportive parts with any particular persons or places in your life? Where do you feel most connected in the cosmos?

Take time, again, to experience the flow of life in and through your whole being, body, mind, and spirit. Visualize this cosmic and microcosmic flow nurturing you and others whom you will never meet. Feel your intimate connection with the universal energy that flows in and through your life. Conclude by giving thanks for the dynamic relatedness of God's life and the body that God inspires.

LIVING ADVENTUROUSLY

Today we expand our gaze to include not only our human and nonhuman companions but also the cosmos. In the course of the day, reflect upon the wider world that gives you life—the moon, planets, sun, and the stars light-years away. Behold the wonder of the earth and the world beyond the earth's atmosphere. Give thanks for the life-giving energies and movements of life beyond this planet. Let it inspire reverence in thought, word, and deed for all things. Commit yourself to becoming a cosmic as well as a planetary citizen.

In Serving Others, We Serve God

[Jesus asked,] "Which of these three, do you think, was a neighbor to the man who fell into the hands of the robbers?" [The lawyer replied,] "The one who showed him mercy."

—Luke 10:36-37

Throughout this book, we have danced around the theological term *panentheism*, the affirmation that God is present in all things, and all things are present in God. Panentheism is to be distinguished from *pantheism*, which asserts that God and the world are one and the same reality. Although the word *panentheism* may be new to your ears, it describes a reality that would have been experientially familiar to Jesus and the Hebrew prophets. At the heart of panentheism is the affirmation that God is as near as your next breath and the next person you meet on the street. All moments reveal God, and all actions live eternally within God's experience of the world. God is in all things, and all things are in God.

Right now, as I write this section, the energy of the wind blowing in and around my back porch, causing half a dozen wind chimes to strike gently, draws my attention to the presence of God in all things. God is in the wind and in my breathing, and also in my deeply felt gratitude for the blessings of this most glorious day and the leisure that enables me to write this morning. The vision of panentheism finds its fulfillment in the life of Jesus the Healer and Teacher and in our own quest to embody the mind and heart of Christ in our lives today. Jesus recognized God's healing and transforming presence as the life-giving force in all things. But Jesus knew that God is more than we can imagine, and in that "more" we, the universe, and our personal lives find their deepest meaning and fulfillment.

Jesus' parable of the good Samaritan reveals the radical nature of "lived omnipresence" that lies at the heart of a panentheistic understanding of reality (Luke 10:25-37). Do you recall the story? While religious leaders pass by a man left beaten on a dangerous road, a Samaritan traveler, scorned by many Jews as an ethnic and religious inferior, stops to lend him aid. The story of this generous outsider reminds us that every moment is a vocational moment in which we may choose to follow or turn away from God's vision for our lives in this place and time. Every moment's encounter is a gift from God and an opportunity to make a difference to God and the world.

Jesus' response to the question "Who is my neighbor?" joins metaphysics, theology, and ethics. The boundary between neighbor and stranger is often defined by our recognition of a common reality, history, and value. If Samaritans and Jews are truly neighbors, then they are also God's beloved children, worthy of love and care. Further, if Samaritan and Jew alike reveal the creativity and care of God, then the only appropriate ethical response is compassion and hospitality. We are one in the Spirit, regardless of differences in age, ethnicity, race, gender, or sexual orientation.

While others may have walked by the wounded man, assuming that their vocation lay in another place and time, the Samaritan discovered his vocation in the here and now by caring for a person who in other circumstances might have seen him as an enemy.

We also live out our vocation in the present moment as well as in the evolving future. The priest and Levite were so purpose-driven that they failed to experience the vocation of the present moment. The priest and Levite could not overcome their own personal and religious agendas and their narrow vision of who was truly included in God's reign to see God's presence in a vulnerable stranger. Nor could they envisage the relationship between this particular moment and God's vision of the human adventure in generations to come.

The Samaritan, in contrast, saw God's calling in the present moment and immediate encounter, even if responding to the wounded traveler meant letting go of his plans for the immediate future. He saw his own wholeness and the well-being of the wounded stranger as one reality. This Samaritan made room in his life for God's unexpected revelations. Although he, like the priest and Levite, had the freedom to say no to God's calling, he chose to be God's partner in healing the world. His act of compassion broke down the barriers of prejudice and hatred and opened the door to reconciliation between at least one Jew and one Samaritan.

Our world is transformed one person and one encounter at a time. Jesus' parable of the good Samaritan weaves together giving and receiving. The wounded Jew had to accept the love he received from a potential enemy in order to complete the circle of love. Vulnerability often breaks down our prejudices. When we discover that we need others, the barriers between "us" and "them" are overcome; in Jesus' story, Jew and Samaritan join in the dance of creative transformation.

I invite you to consider Jesus' question, "Who is your neighbor?" (paraphrase of verse 36). He or she may not be the one you expect your neighbor to be. While there are no absolute guidelines to neighborliness, adventurous living awakens us to the holiness of each moment and the divine presence in every stranger. Remember, your neighbor is your companion in God's circle of love.

A Prayer for the Adventure

O God of creation, hold all things in your circle of love. Wind and trees, friends and enemies, and intimates and strangers hold all things in the circle of your love. Hold me in the circle of your love that I might be bold in my loving and creative in caring. From the circle of love, loving myself as you love me, let me love without measure or fear. Amen.

CHOOSING YOUR OWN AFFIRMATION

Vision and affirmation are interconnected. Throughout the day, it helps to remind yourself that you are always in the presence of holiness, whether you are bathing in the beauty of the sunrise, petting a companion animal, caressing a loved one, or greeting a stranger.

- All persons are my neighbors.
- I see God in every encounter.

- I reach out in love to both strangers and enemies.
- I reach out in love to (*an unexpected person*).

YOUR HOLY IMAGINATION

In this meditation, you will live imaginatively with Jesus' parable of the good Samaritan. Take a moment to relax in God's presence, breathing in harmony with God's healing breath.

Visualize yourself embarking on a journey. You may be walking or driving. Where are you going—are you headed to an appointment? a class? a friend's house? Visualize the scene and the route you are taking.

As you continue on your journey, you notice a person in need. What is her or his problem? How do you feel when you see this person's need? Do you stop and help? If so, what actions do you perform to support him or her? (If you pass by, what is your reason for not stopping? How does your life change because of your choice not to stop?)

If you choose to stop and provide help, imagine what happens next. How do you support the one in need? How do you provide for her or his well-being, both short- and long-term? How do you conclude this holy encounter?

Whether or not you help the one in need, take time to give God thanks for synchronous encounters that give you the opportunity to reach out to others.

LIVING ADVENTUROUSLY

An adventurous life is a visionary life in which we are constantly on the lookout for divine inspirations in persons and situations. If God is in all things, then every occasion mediates inspiration and holiness to us. There are no separate givers and receivers but a fabric of destiny that calls all of us to creativity and love in relationship to one another.

As your day unfolds, keep your eyes open. Listen for the calling of the present moment. Your vocation may call to you in something as simple as responding to an e-mail or a text message, or noticing the distressed expression of one of your household companions as you walk out the door, or witnessing an accident on the road, or seeing a friend or colleague under stress. When such encounters occur, prayerfully open to God's guidance about how you can join your well-being with theirs. As you feel called, respond to the need in light of your other responsibilities and need to care for your own or your family's well-being.

I must admit that this may be a challenging practice. I struggle internally with inviting homeless persons to my home and usually end up either giving them money or referring them to a shelter instead. As a child of the 1960s, I feel ambivalence whenever I pass a hitchhiker, even though I know that I am also called to care for my own safety and my responsibilities to my family. I struggle regularly with the possibility of becoming a prudent yet good Samaritan.

DAY 25

In Christ We Are One

Holy Father, protect them in your name that you have given me, so that they may be one, as we are one.
— John 17:11

John 17 presents a stunning integration of theology, spirituality, and ethics that challenges the individualistic and dualistic worldview that is so characteristic of the modern era. As he blesses his disciples then and now, Jesus describes his relationship with God as the model for the divine-human relationship: "The glory that you have given me I have given them, so that they may be one, as we are one, I in them and you in me, that they may become completely one, so that the world may know that you have sent me and have loved them even as you have loved me" (John 17:22-23).

These words describe both a theological reality and a spiritual awareness. Whether or not we are aware of it, we are one with God, Christ, and one another. This metaphysical vision blends uniqueness and diversity with interrelatedness and unity. God is our deepest reality, guiding and inspiring us to join personal fulfillment with planetary healing. Our awareness of our spiritual unity with others is not the result of the external descent of an alien spirit, psychological transference, or ecstatic worship but an enlivened awareness of what is always the case—God is in us and we are in God. As the Prayer of Saint Patrick proclaims:

Christ behind and before me,
Christ beneath and above me,
Christ with me and in me,
Christ around and about me,
Christ on my left and my right.[3]

The nature of this holy relationship will always remain mysterious, but what it points to is the deep awareness that our moment-by-moment experience is shaped by the intricate interdependence of the universe and the God who moves within all things, joining them with one another in love.

This dynamic theological vision has profound ethical and spiritual consequences. It inspires us to affirm that in a world of diversity, multiplicity, and uniqueness, there is no "other." This is at the heart of Peter's mystical vision in Acts 10. After protesting God's command that he eat from a bountiful buffet of forbidden foods, Peter experienced divine inspiration in the words *call nothing profane*. In the fabric of relationships, we create each other's experience moment by moment. The fates of a Middle Eastern despot, Iraqi religious and political leaders, homeless families in New Orleans, and trapped miners in West Virginia shape who I am and my possibilities for the future. My faithfulness to my wife shapes my adult child's vision of marriage and relationships with women. My honesty in filing my income taxes or returning money left in an ATM machine creates a ripple effect across the universe that promotes an environment of greater trust and community. Your spiritual and ethical integrity shapes countless others' as well.

In his prayers of farewell and blessing, Jesus challenges individualistic and dualistic views of economics, medicine, politics, spirituality, and embodiment. He calls us to love God in the world of the flesh and love the stranger whose face we see only on the evening news. He calls us to see the earth as a lively community of relationships in which every part is joined, despite apparent self-interest, competition, and conflict.

Rippling across the centuries through our congregations, personal devotions, and deeply felt spirituality, Jesus' first-century prayer still makes a difference in our lives. Jesus' prayer shapes our own sense of God's presence in our lives and inspires us to see God in all things and all things in God.

A Prayer for the Adventure

Holy One, give me vision to see you in all things, and all things in your love. Let me see Christ in all things and all things in Christ. Let me love Christ in all things and receive Christ's love through all things. Let your vision abound in all things, transforming the world and transforming my heart. Amen.

CHOOSING YOUR OWN AFFIRMATION

I must admit that I have to constantly remind myself of the unity of life. Frankly, I find the tension of self-*centeredness* and *self*-centeredness most challenging in my own family relationships, personal economics, and workplace decision making where I am tempted to live by a "zero sum" worldview in which your gain is my loss, rather than an "abundant life" worldview in which everyone prospers together. Throughout the day, I have to take a breath and remind myself to let go beyond my small self and its defensiveness to claim my larger spiritual self whose stature embraces holy otherness and planetary well-being in a "win-win" mentality. Prayerful affirmations remind me of who I am and of the holy reality that joins all things.

- In Christ, I am joined with all creation.
- My well-being and the well-being of the planet are one.
- I am one with my brothers and sisters in Christ.
- I am one in the Spirit with (*name a particular person*).
- I am joined with (*name a particular person from another Christian tradition*).

YOUR HOLY IMAGINATION

In this exercise in holy imagination, begin by reading John 17:22-23. Let the words sink in, absorbing their insight and wisdom. Hear them being addressed specifically to you in your world.

Visualize yourself simply being where you are today—spiritually, physically, geographically. With each breath imagine you are inhaling the presence of God. Picture Christ's presence growing within you. (In truth, we are not really invoking God or Christ by breath prayers, since God's presence is intimate and universal, and wells up within us, giving life to each thought and emotion, each cell and organ.)

Centered in your experience of God in your life, begin to imagine those persons, related or not, that you call your family. Visualize your connectedness with them with each breath. Breathe in their lives and exhale your love for them.

Joined with your family and God, think of your connectedness with your community of faith or spiritual community of friends with each breath. Breathe in their lives and exhale your love for them. Visualize your unity with Christians of all traditions. Breathe in their lives and exhale your love for them.

Imagine one person who represents the world beyond your nation or the Christian tradition. Joined with God, your family, and your spiritual community, breathe in her or his life, and breathe out your love for him or her.

Visualize the whole earth, intricately bound together in one fabric of relatedness. See the boundaries of nations flowing into one another. Experience the peoples of the world woven together in one family. Joined with God, your family, your community of faith, your spiritual community, and a beloved stranger, breathe in the world in all its wonder, and exhale your love for the world, part and whole.

Conclude this imaginative prayer by once again focusing your attention from the whole to the part—from the world, to the stranger from another land, to Christians everywhere, to the spiritual community, to your family, and finally to yourself as a center of divine life.

LIVING ADVENTUROUSLY

Today we commit ourselves to awareness of the power of our thoughts to shape the world in which we live. Knowing that our thoughts and words radiate across the universe, shaping the experiences of others and the well-being of the planet, we are called to be mindful of the quality of our thoughts, words, and emotions. The transformed mind is one whose thoughts, emotions, and words are healing and unifying, even amid conflict. We can educate our emotions just as we can educate our thoughts through observation, affirmations, spiritual friendships, and therapeutic relationships.

Take time to pause and notice your thoughts, words, and emotions. Observe times when your words are characterized by isolated individualism, zero-sum scarcity thinking, violence, and self-centeredness. Without judgment, pause for a moment to notice your tendency to isolate, polarize, and condemn other persons. Remind yourself of your constant unity with Christ and all creation. Let your words throughout the day promote healing and unity with everyone you meet.

DAY 26

We Respond to the Cries of Creation

Creation waits with eager longing for the revealing of the children of God.

—Romans 8:19

Once again we return to the broader themes of creation. As a result of the negative impact of theologies of dominion and destruction, we must constantly remind ourselves that the biblical tradition is profoundly creation-affirming. Salvation is not just about humankind and its relationship to God but encompasses the whole planet. Sin is not just turning from God and our human neighbors but also the destruction of animal species, the water and soil, and now the fragile atmosphere that supports and protects life on earth. Today, Christian ethics, salvation, and spirituality must embrace the planet as well as our human neighbors. This is simply good biblical theology. An omnipresent and omniactive God centers all things, not just humankind or particular human beings. When we move beyond anthropocentric thinking and action, we discover that all creation is alive with God's presence and that we have a role in healing the earth as well as ourselves.

Paul's planetary vision in Romans 8 is breathtaking in scope. God is moving within our hearts and souls, whispering to us in every breath. God is also moving in all creation. The universe is the birthing room of divine creativity, and all creation lives in hope of actualizing its role in a community that embraces God and all creatures.

Wholeness and brokenness characterize the nonhuman as well as human world. Created for relationship, creation cries out in pain. While we need not emphasize original sin as the source of human and nonhuman pain, it is clear that humankind is responsible for much of the pain and destruction in the world, especially among nonhuman species. Creation cries out for wholeness. But are we listening?

The experience of pain, some ethicists suggest, is the basis of moral sensitivity. We cannot achieve the "beloved community" envisaged by Martin Luther King Jr. without eliminating needless suffering. "Life is robbery," as philosopher Alfred North Whitehead notes, but our killing and experimentation must be justified by the achievement of significant benefits to humankind and nonhuman creatures. We must give thanks for all the animals that have been sacrificed for our well-being, while committing ourselves to preventing needless future animal suffering.

The vision of Romans 8 places our lives in planetary and cosmic perspective. We cry out for God, and so does all creation. Creation awaits new birth, but so do we—not just as "spiritual beings" but as planetary citizens. The Spirit moves in sighs too deep for words, inspiring us to prayerful contemplation and service. That same Spirit is prayerfully moving in the nonhuman world. Biblical ethics reminds us that intelligence and rationality are not the only criteria for a relationship with God. To place this limit on the divine-human relationship would be to deny God's presence in persons with Down syndrome, Alzheimer's disease, and reversible and irreversible comas, as well as in fetuses and infants.

As I have stated throughout this book, God is present in all things from dolphins to Siamese cats. God hears all cries and wordless prayers for mercy and relief, whether they come from hungry children, abandoned animals, or persons marginalized because of race, gender, or sexual orientation.

Hearing the groaning of creation—in humankind and in the nonhuman world—is heartbreaking. But the groans of creation are symphonic as well as tragic. They are signs of birth as well as death. As we pause and listen with our whole selves, new melodies fill our minds and warm our hearts as all creation joins in a hymn of praise.

> Praise [God], sun and moon;
>> praise [God], all you shining stars!
> Praise [God], you highest heavens,
>> and you waters above the heavens. . . .
> Mountains and all hills,
>> fruit trees and all cedars!
> Wild animals and all cattle,
>> creeping things and flying birds! . . .
> Young men and women alike,
>> old and young together! (Psalm 148:3-4, 9-10, 12)

A Prayer for the Adventure

Holy Adventure, whose Spirit breathes through all life and enlivens the cells of our bodies and the birds of the air, open us to your life in all things. Help us to experience the deep cries of creation. Help us to feel the pain of vanishing species, of dying forests, of melting ice caps, of threatened generations of unborn creatures. Help us to be your partners in healing the earth, in restoring life where we have been agents of destruction, of giving hope to generations beyond us who will dwell, both human and nonhuman alike, on this good earth. In Christ's name. Amen.

CHOOSING YOUR OWN AFFIRMATION

By enabling us to experience our theology with our whole selves, affirmations open us to God's new creation in ourselves and in the world. As a spiritual practice, affirmations train us to "see" God's hand everywhere and to take our place as God's partners in healing the earth.

- I experience God in the voices of the earth.
- I listen for the cries of creation.
- I listen for God in the pain and beauty of the nonhuman world.
- I listen for God in (*an animal in pain or in the delight of an animal*).

YOUR HOLY IMAGINATION

Take a few minutes to read Romans 8:18-28 once again. Listen deeply for your own inner groaning and the groaning of the nonhuman world. Visualize your connectedness with the whole earth. Experience the pain of the nonhuman world. Embrace that pain as part of your own life. Imagine the faces of nonhuman creatures.

Visualize the nonhuman world at play and creativity. Imagine God's Spirit moving through every creature, giving it life, love, hope, and joy. See God in all things and all things in God as you visualize our planet as one great, interconnected life.

LIVING ADVENTUROUSLY

Today I invite you to continue affirming the whole earth as God's creation. In the last few days, our focus has been the interplay of the human and nonhuman worlds as an antidote to human-centered visions of ethics and salvation. When we disregard the earth and nonhuman species, we contribute to our own destruction and the destruction of our home planet. A relational vision of God and the world sees salvation and wholeness as embracing all things, not just humankind.

If you are part of a community of faith, raise issues of the relationship between faith and ecology. Invite your congregation to have a service involving the blessing of animals or celebrating Earth Day. Take time to consider the relationship between your diet and lifestyle and the well-being of creation. In what ways can you simplify your life and make your life less destructive of the natural world? Today embody one practice that affirms the unity of all life and nurtures your spirit—such as walking rather than driving, having a meatless lunch, eating range-fed rather than grain-fed beef, turning down your thermostat and wearing a sweater indoors. These are small acts, but when multiplied by millions, they can help us become God's partners in healing the world.

DAY 27

We Serve God by "Considering the Lilies"

Consider the lilies of the field, how they grow; they neither toil nor spin, yet I tell you, even Solomon in all his glory was not clothed like one of these.

—Matthew 6:28-29

The world of nature fills our lives with beauty. Each morning I feast my eyes on the sunrise, the meadow that borders our neighborhood, and the flight of migrating birds. Wildflowers and pastures bathe our eyes in beauty. I have been awestruck by moose and bison in Yellowstone. In such moments, we can surely "taste and see that the LORD is good" (Ps. 34:8).

Reflecting on Jesus' words from the Sermon on the Mount, Martin Luther asserted that the lilies of the field and the birds of the air are God's teachers to anxious human beings. Utterly dependent on forces beyond their control, the birds of the air trust God to supply their needs. Simply by being themselves without artificial adornment, the lilies of the field possess a beauty that humbles human cosmetology and tailoring.

God reveals beauty and care in and through all things. Divine care will provide for our deepest needs for today and tomorrow.

The simple wonders of creation, the gifts of God that we can neither control nor enhance, invite us to wonder, appreciation, and reverence. The galaxies and solar systems spin throughout space without our efforts. The faithful day-to-day rising and setting of the sun do not require our strategic planning, "best practices," or purpose drivenness. The ever-present fidelity of God invites us to nurture graceful playfulness even as we seek to bring healing and justice to the earth. Trusting in God's abundant care, we pray with our Native American brothers and sisters:

> I walk with beauty before me.
> I walk with beauty behind me.
> I walk with beauty above me.
> I walk with beauty below me.
> I walk with beauty all around me.
> Your world is so beautiful, O God.

A Prayer for the Adventure

Artist of Becoming, whose beauty bathes my senses, let all my days be filled with wonder and gratitude, and let the beauty I experience inspire me to acts of loving beauty to all creation. Amen.

CHOOSING YOUR OWN AFFIRMATION

Albert Schweitzer spoke of the importance of reverence for life in all its varied forms. To simply exist is to be a locus of value, worthy of respect, honor, and reverence. Spiritual affirmations open our senses to the wonder and holiness of the nonhuman world as a revelation of God's creativity.

- I experience wonder and beauty everywhere I look.
- I walk with beauty all around me.
- I experience and reverence God's presence in (*a place of beauty*).

- I trust God's care in all things.
- I trust God's care in (*a challenging situation*).

YOUR HOLY IMAGINATION

Begin this exercise by relaxing in God's care. Take a few moments simply to experience your breath and the wonder of your embodiment. Then take time to remember a place of beauty. (It may be the Grand Canyon, the Pacific or Atlantic Ocean, a sunrise, or your own backyard. This morning, as I practiced this meditation, my mind turned to the Cliff Walk in Newport, Rhode Island, which joins the grandeur of the ocean with the creativity of human architecture.) Visualize the calm and wonder of that place. Experience the joy of right where you belong in the universe. Put yourself in that holy space, rejoicing and resting in God's abundant sufficiency and care that sustains and empowers you.

Whenever you feel overwhelmed by stress, return to that beautiful spot as a place of retreat, refreshment, and recreation. Visualize its wonder and beauty and the graceful care of God. Know that you are always bathed in divine beauty, and that inner peace is just a moment away.

LIVING ADVENTUROUSLY

In this meditation, simply bathe your experience in beauty. Theologian and author Patricia Adams Farmer encourages us to take regular "beauty breaks" throughout the day.[4] These beauty breaks can be times spent walking outdoors or in human-made beauty spots as we open ourselves to beauty and wonder without any sense of purpose, or they might involve listening to the wind chimes tinkling on the porch or playing catch with a child. These purposeless moments in which we "neither toil nor spin" (Matt. 6:28) provide relaxation, ground us in the nonhuman world, and awaken us to the wonder that undergirds every moment of life. We can in every moment, with Julian of Norwich, experience God's loving care in "something small, no bigger than a hazelnut," and know that God cares for us as well.

Praise God with All Creation

Let everything that breathes praise the LORD*!*

—Psalm 150:6

A ccording to the biblical tradition, the nonhuman world groans, but it also teaches, praises, and plays. Pause for a moment now and read Psalms 148–150 imaginatively. You will experience an eternal hymn of praise welling up from all creation and from your own inner life. Every created thing rejoices in the wonder of life, and deep down, so do you!

Yes, creation groans, teaches, praises, and plays. Creation reflects the passion, wisdom, wonder, joy, and playfulness of divine creativity.

Authentic praise wells up in the joy of experiencing the fullness of our lives in concert with all creation. God does not need our praise, like a ruthless or imperialistic potentate, to bolster a narcissistic or fragile ego. Rather, we need to praise God in order to attune ourselves with the rhythms of universal love and creativity and to experience God's own joyful song in our uplifted voices.

I believe that we praise God best by rejoicing in our lives and sharing our joy of life through acts of generosity, kindness, and hospitality. We praise the Creator by becoming creators ourselves and appreciating the wonder of God's creativity in ourselves and in the world. We praise God by being fully alive to the beauty and wonder of our unique and precious life and the uniqueness and wonder of all things.

In a world that reflects God's artistry at every turn, the glory of God is also reflected in the lilies of field, the twinkling stars, the color purple, the flowing river, and the howling wolf. Listen to the words of the following hymn, adapted from the poetry of Saint Francis of Assisi:

All creatures of our God and King,
lift up your voice and with us sing;

Alleluia, Alleluia!
O burning sun with golden beam,
O silver moon with softer gleam,
O praise God, O praise God,
Alleluia, Alleluia, Alleluia!

O rushing wind with voice so strong,
you clouds that sail in heav'n along,
O praise God, Alleluia!
O rising morn, in praise rejoice,
you lights of evening find a voice,
O praise God, O praise God,
Alleluia, Alleluia, Alleluia!

O flowing water, pure and clear,
make music for your God to hear,
Alleluia, Alleluia!
O blazing fire who lights the night,
providing warmth, enhancing sight,
O praise God, O praise God,
Alleluia, Alleluia, Alleluia![5]

Creation dances and plays with the One whose holy adventure brings forth life in every moment. We find our joy and place in the universe by claiming our proper vocation as lively and creative participants in the evolving universe. As God's beloved children in a world of beloved creatures, we can rejoice in creative partnership with all things. With every breath, we can experience the wonder of life and the community of all living things. We can breathe and dance and laugh with the Holy Adventurer and our adventurous companions on this good earth. "Let everything that breathes praise the LORD!"

A Prayer for the Adventure

In silence, O God, we breathe. In silence, we pray. In silence, we open to your breath in our breath, enlivening, inspiring, awakening, creating, and healing. Breathe in and through us that we might breathe out your joy, healing, and love as partners in your Holy Breath. Amen.

Choosing Your Own Affirmation

Joy is a gift of grace and self-awareness. In a cultural and religious tradition that often exalts the discontinuity of humankind and nature, global mysticism is matter of vision and practice. Wonder is cultivated as well as received.

One of my favorite prayers comes from the Shalem Institute for Spiritual Formation in Bethesda, Maryland.[6] The following words may be sung or chanted and adapted as a grateful response to any life situation.

I thank you, God, for the won-der of my be - ing.

Chant by Isabella Bates. Used by permission.

- I thank you, God, for the wonder of all being.
- I thank you, God, for the wonder of (*your child, parent, life companion, or friend*).
- I thank you, God, for the wonder of (*a fellow creature*).

To awaken your senses, you may also choose a holy affirmation such as:

- I breathe joy with all creation.
- Every breath praises God.
- I laugh with God at life's hilarity.
- I skip and dance in love and wonder.

Your Holy Imagination

In this imaginative prayer, take a few moments to read Psalms 148–150 once again. Let these psalms flood your heart and mind. Breathe deeply as you ponder your relatedness to all things. Imagine a lively, energetic breath blowing through all things and through your finite, unique, and precious life. Visualize this breath encircling the earth and giving life to every creature. Picture the singing birds, running deer, and lilies of the field breathing and praising God. Imagine the human family enlivened by this lively breath. Let this breath enliven and inspire you in this time of meditation and throughout the day.

LIVING ADVENTUROUSLY

We praise God by acts of joyful gratitude. In every encounter, breathe your gratitude for each and every thing. Thank God for the wonders of creation and share that thanks in your appreciation for the unique beauty of all things.

As the occasion permits, voice your gratitude in hymn, praise, gesture, or shared thanksgiving. Take time today to sing your faith. Let each breath be one of praise, thanksgiving, and love. Say "thank you" to the birds of the air, the stars above, your companion animals, and for every simple gesture of support and love.

HEALING
ADVENTURES

I hope that by now you have discovered that adventurous living involves becoming God's partner in consciously healing your life, relationships, and the world. Your task is preventative and responsive, and individual and corporate. On the one hand, our faith calls us to nurture our temple of the Holy Spirit through practices of mindfulness, care, spiritual formation, and justice. On the other hand, the realities of personal, relational, and community disease, alienation, and injustice challenge us also to heal the earth, in part and in whole. Like physicians of both the East and West, we are called to respond to our personal and social malaise through disciplined practices of healing, restoration, and transformation. Fortunately, many of the spiritual practices that promote wellness also enable us to recover our wholeness as persons and communities.

The quest for healing is flourishing throughout the church and the secular world. With recent developments in global medicine and global spirituality, persons are integrating traditional Western forms of medicine and complementary modalities such as acupuncture, Reiki, therapeutic touch, massage, homeopathy, diet, yoga, qigong (sometimes spelled chi kung), and tai chi. Western medical researchers are discovering that traditional spiritual practices of prayer, healing touch, meditation, forgiveness, and active community participation contribute to physical well-being, mental health, and

148

longevity. The Newtonian, mechanistic, and dualistic worldview that provided the intellectual foundation for Western medicine is being challenged in laboratories as well as in medical practices and personal experiences.

In a similar vein, both mainstream and progressive Christians are rediscovering the healing ministry of Jesus and his challenge to his followers to do "greater things" (John 14:12, NIV) in healing the world. When we begin consciously to experience the world in terms of relationship, interdependence, and community, the healing stories of the New Testament come alive intellectually, spiritually, and physically. Miracles happen!

God's passion for wholeness energizes and animates the impulse for well-being in our cells, immune system, and emotional lives. While most of the time the quest for healing in an organism or a system, like the growth of a mustard seed, is gradual and undramatic, now and then the interplay of God's presence, human openness, and supportive healing relationships brings forth miracles, or "acts of power" in which healing processes are accelerated. Such moments are not violations of the evolving and interdependent laws of nature but revelations of the "more" that resides in every situation.

> God's passion for wholeness energizes and animates the impulse for well-being in our cells, immune system, and emotional lives.

In the week ahead, we will intentionally explore the meaning of divine healing in our lives. When we choose to be conscious partners in God's healing adventure, we awaken to practices that transform our minds, bodies, spirits, and communities. We find relief from pain, as well as new energy and physical restoration. We also may experience greater patience with health conditions that cannot be alleviated by prayer or medication alone. From this perspective, healing and wholeness are not magic; rather, in the lively matrix of events, God is always seeking the healing that brings peace and well-being to our environment and to ourselves. At times, this may mean a peaceful and faithful death rather than a dramatic reversal of a terminal illness. But with God as our intimate companion, when there cannot be a cure of physical symptoms, there can always be a healing of the spirit.

Loving God
in the World of the Flesh

God saw everything that [God] had made, and indeed, it was very good.

—Genesis 1:31

he healing adventure begins with affirming our essential embodiment. "And it was very good," proclaims the Genesis creation story. Embodiment, sexuality, and relationships alike reveal divine creativity and wisdom. The Gospel of John's creation story proclaims that "the Word became flesh and lived among us" (John 1:14). Divine creativity permeates every dimension of reality. The heavens declare the glory of God, and so do our immune, cardiovascular, digestive, and reproductive systems. Whether young or old, slender or obese, wrinkled or smooth, our bodies reveal God's loving handiwork.

Paul's affirmation that the body is "a temple of the Holy Spirit" is a call to see our bodies as media of divine revelation, worthy of love and care (1 Cor. 6:19). We love God in the world of the flesh by treating our own bodies and others' bodies in ways that promote healing and wholeness.

Adventurous spirituality embraces the wonder and beauty of all things, including our bodies. Regardless of our health condition, we can experience God's adventure moving in our own flesh and blood. We can rejoice in divine inspiration embodied within every heartbeat and thought, and we can recognize that as God's beloved children, our faith embraces our bodies as well as our minds, spirits, and relationships.

A Prayer for the Adventure

Spirit of the living God, inspire me with each breath. When I reflect on the body that is your temple, I confess that I have turned from health to disease by my diet, lifestyle, and attitudes. I have not loved your temple with holy love, nor have I loved the temples of others. I have forgotten the basic needs of others and the interdependence of our bodies. Help me to live well and simply, to eat with gratitude, and to share my bounty so others might simply live and then live well and better by your grace. Amen.

CHOOSING YOUR OWN AFFIRMATION

In a culture that often devalues certain bodies and identifies sin with sexuality and ugliness with aging and disability, we are challenged to experience the beauty of our bodies from God's perspective. Through our affirmations, we challenge and still the voices of our culture and our own bodily self-deprecation, and we learn to embrace our bodies just as they are—the first step to experiencing health and wholeness.

- My body is the temple of God.
- My body is beautiful.
- Aging brings greater beauty to my mind, body, and spirit.
- My (*a particular part of my body*) is beautiful.
- I love God by caring for my body in a healthy way.

YOUR HOLY IMAGINATION

Our bodies in their intricate beauty reveal divine wisdom. In this exercise, we experience divine wisdom as moving within our embodiment. In the stillness, breathe in the presence of divine wisdom. With each breath, imagine God's light entering your body, filling it with healing light from the top of your head to the soles of your feet. Visualize God's healing light enlivening your immune, cardiovascular, circulatory, digestive, and reproductive systems. Imagine your face reflecting divine wisdom and beauty. Experience God's light radiating from your whole being. You are a living, breathing temple of God.

Now ponder a friend, spouse, partner, or child. Visualize God's light flowing through every cell of this person's body and whole being. See this individual as revealing divinity in her or his embodiment. Experience that person as healthy and whole—and remember that she or he is a living, breathing temple of God.

Next, think about someone who fails to measure up to your own or our society's vision of beauty. (This may be a person with disabilities, an older adult, a person with Down syndrome, an obese person. It may simply be someone who does not fall into any category but whom you do not consider attractive.) Visualize God's light flowing in and through that person. See that person as God's beloved child, revealing God in his or her embodiment. Imagine the person as healthy and whole—and recognize that he or she too is a living, breathing temple of God.

LIVING ADVENTUROUSLY

Our attitudes toward our bodies and others' bodies often reflect the social nature of sin. Our social attitudes may diminish the personhood of others and lead us to treat them as less than fully human. Unconsciously, virtually all of us are conditioned by our society's negative attitudes toward embodiment. We become liberated from the sins of our society through mindful self-examination, which eventually changes our attitudes and behavior toward others.

Throughout the day, be attentive to your "self-talk" as it relates to your own embodiment and the embodiment of others. How often do you look at yourself or others in terms of beauty or judgment? In what way do you see others' bodies—as temples of God or as places of ugliness? How do you judge your own embodiment? Do you affirm the wonder of your body just as it is?

In light of your self-examination, will you commit yourself to affirming the wholeness of others, regardless of age, weight, physical appearance, or sexual orientation? Will you commit yourself to affirming the bodies of others through involvement in actions that promote economic justice and physical well-being, especially for those who have experienced economic inequality or social judgment as a result of their health or appearance?

DAY 30

We Can Glorify God in Our Bodies

Glorify God in your body.

—1 Corinthians 6:20

Glorify God in your body! What we do with our bodies really matters. As temples of God, our bodies reveal God's creativity and wisdom. Our thoughts and emotions radiate throughout the body, and our physical well-being and chemical balance shape our thinking and feeling as well. While we may inherit certain characteristics and tendencies (genetic, body type, metabolism, strengths, and weaknesses), we are not the victims of our genetic and biological inheritance. We can, with God's help, be artists of our embodiment by intentionally loving and caring for our bodies.

The story of Naaman, a powerful military leader who was stricken with a skin ailment, reminds us that some of the most helpful ways to care for our bodies are right in front of us (2 Kings 5:1-14). In the encounter of Naaman and Elisha, the military leader becomes angry when Elisha asks him to dip himself in the Jordan River seven times rather than prescribing an exotic cure or a visit to a distant spa. Naaman's path to healing is simple and readily available. This is also true for us. God's healing touch is available right where we are, and we can access divine power at any moment. But often we don't see it or want it!

While we cannot guarantee good health of body, mind, and spirit, we can commit ourselves to healing practices that promote wellness at every level of our being. The pathway to wholeness is spiritual as well as ethical and behavioral. We are the stewards of our own embodiment, and the way we use our bodies reflects our self-awareness and personal values. Without going into great detail, we can glorify God by:

1. *moving with the Spirit* (physical practices such as yoga, qigong, tai chi, walking, jogging, swimming)
2. *spiritual practices* (meditation, prayer, silence) that not only align us with God but also replenish and refresh our bodies
3. *holy eating* (eating our food with gratitude, discovering what is good for us, eating with self-awareness, and eating ethically—in other words, eating foods whose production does not destroy the environment or contribute to unjust economic or working conditions)
4. *sabbath keeping* (taking time to trust God by taking a day for study, refreshment, and worship each week)
5. *loving relationships* (finding creative ways to nurture our relationships with others)
6. *service* (reaching out to others in committed and healthy ways—medical studies suggest that persons who volunteer not only experience greater health and happiness but also the "helper's high")
7. *healing communities* (committing ourselves to a healthy Christian community that nurtures our well-being and supports our commitments)
8. *healing touch* (massage, Reiki, therapeutic touch, hugs, physical intimacy)

We glorify God by loving ourselves as we truly are and, out of that of that healthy self-affirmation, reaching out in service to others. In the movie *Chariots of Fire*, Olympic runner Eric Liddell saw long-distance running as part of his Christian vocation and as a means of sharing his faith. Liddell revealed his vision of glorifying God with his body when he affirmed, "[God] . . . made me fast. And when I run, I feel His pleasure." What gives you authentic pleasure? When do you feel God's liveliness coursing through your body?

With every breath we can affirm, "Let everything that breathes praise the LORD!" (Ps. 150:6). We can rejoice in the simplest physical sensations. Let your actions and care for yourself and others glorify God in your body.

A Prayer for the Adventure

God of change and glory, God of young and old, let me glorify you
with each breath. Let me praise you with each footstep. Let each meal
be a prayer and each touch bring healing. Nourished by your gifts, I
joyfully nourish others, sharing the grace I have received through the
Healer of Nazareth. Amen.

CHOOSING YOUR OWN AFFIRMATION

Caring for ourselves and others is a matter of intentionality and choice.
Affirmations enable us to be more conscious of our behavior and support
our quest for personal wholeness and ethical living.

- I glorify God in my body.
- I reflect my love for God and myself in a healthy lifestyle.
- I eat healthy foods that contribute to my own well-being and the
  well-being of others.
- I glorify God by (*name a certain behavior practice*).
- God made me (*name a characteristic of yourself*), and when I (*name
  an action*), I feel God's pleasure.

YOUR HOLY IMAGINATION

Take time today to be still in God's presence, experiencing God's healing
light with every breath. Feel God's light bathing you in health and wholeness from head to toe. If there are any places of disease, imagine God's light
focusing on these places.

As you live in God's light, visualize your own spiritual and physical
well-being, regardless of your current health condition. Ask God where you
need to grow in terms of your health and fitness. What insights do you
receive? Visualize yourself participating in these practices of health and fitness. Picture God's joy and energy flowing through your life. See your own
well-being contributing to the well-being of others.

LIVING ADVENTUROUSLY

You can glorify God in many ways. You can care for your unique body and commit yourself to practices of wholeness. You can reach out to others with acts of love. You can live and eat ethically and spiritually. A spiritual motto for our time is "Live simply so others can simply live." Where are you called to simplify your eating or lifestyle? Take time to explore the connection between your diet, lifestyle, values, and the economic and social well-being of others. Ponder how your lifestyle shapes the health of the environment in our own country and around the world. Commit yourself to a lifestyle that glorifies God by its care for your human and nonhuman companions.

DAY 31

We Share in God's Healing Touch

[The woman with the hemorrhage said to herself,] "If I but touch his clothes, I will be made well." . . . She felt in her body that she was healed of her disease. Immediately aware that power had gone forth from him, Jesus turned about in the crowd and said, "Who touched my clothes?"

—Mark 5:28-30

Jesus the Healer transformed persons' lives by touching and being touched. Jesus took Peter's mother-in-law by the hand and cured her debilitating fever. Jesus placed a mixture of saliva and dirt on a blind man's eyes, and he regained his sight. Jesus touched the leper, restoring him in body, mind, spirit, relationships, and social position. A woman who had suffered from a gynecological ailment touched Jesus in faith, and the bleeding stopped. A dynamic energy flowed forth from Jesus that transformed her life.

Today, at a time when we are highly conscious of the importance of "safe" touch, we are also discovering the power of appropriate and welcome touch to heal body, mind, and spirit. Jesus' healing touch is being rediscovered in light of the growing influence of complementary medicine in the Western world. It is no coincidence that Christians and non-Christians alike experience greater spiritual and physical wholeness through practices such as healing touch, Reiki, therapeutic touch, and massage therapy.[1] But Christians are also claiming the power of Jesus' healing touch through healing rituals involving the laying on of hands, anointing, and intercessory prayer.[2] The integration of contemporary modalities of healing touch with traditional rituals of healing and other spiritual practices requires Christians to affirm "not less, but a different kind of touch."[3]

In our times "high tech" must be balanced by "high touch" in spiritual practices as well as medical care. As the largest organ of the body, the skin must receive the same intentional and loving care as the heart or immune system if we are to be truly healthy.

For two decades, I have been active in both traditional healing rituals and in the practice of a prayerful form of laying on hands known as Reiki. I believe that we pray with our hands as well as our hearts and minds. Gentle touch extended with an intention of promoting the well-being of another receives and directs the divine energy of wholeness and vitality that resides in all things. I believe that healing energy flowed from Jesus' hands and body, and it also flows from our own lives when we commit ourselves to be God's instruments of healing and wholeness.

In a world in which violent and abusive touch can leave permanent wounds on the spirit as well as the body, Christians are called to practice healing touch with great care and discipline. Healing touch can be mediated by something as simple as a handshake, the passing of the peace, a massage or Reiki treatment, the laying on of hands and anointing with oil in a worship service, and through simple acts of personal and professional support such as hugs and pats on the back or the shoulder. Such touch is inspired by our desire to be God's healing partners in our relationship with others. We can commit ourselves to safe, welcome, hospitable, and life-affirming touch. We can also commit ourselves to protecting vulnerable persons—and, in truth, we all are vulnerable—from manipulative, predatory, and demeaning touch.

Touch can heal. The largest organ of our body (skin) needs healing and affirming touch. Prayerfully connected with God, our touch can be a medium of God's healing touch in the world one person at a time.

A Prayer for the Adventure

Healing God, we open to your healing touch. Awaken us to places where we have chosen disease rather than health, distress rather than peace, busyness rather than calm. Inspire us to live fully, healthfully, and lovingly. Let our every touch bring life and love and healing as we journey with your healing Child, Jesus. Amen.

CHOOSING YOUR OWN AFFIRMATION

As Christians, we are called to be "little Christs" to others. Christ's aim is to reflect God's love in every encounter. Affirmations remind us of the larger context of our actions and our aspiration to be God's partners in healing the world.

- I mediate God's healing touch in every encounter.
- I touch only when it is appropriate and helpful to others.
- I touch with love and healing.
- I touch (*a particular person in your life*) with love and healing.
- I protect vulnerable persons from unhealthy touch.

YOUR HOLY IMAGINATION

In this healing meditation, we receive God's healing touch imaginatively. Take time to be still in God's presence. Breathe deeply and slowly, grounding your energy and opening to God's healing power. With every breath, experience God's healing energy filling your body from head to toe. Feel the divine healing presence, especially in those parts of your life that are in need of wholeness.

In your imagination take a moment to invite Jesus to become your healing partner. Visualize yourself in a place of beauty and calm, such as the forest, the seashore, or the desert. Experience the wonder and beauty of that particular place. Now imagine that Jesus is sitting or walking beside you. The two of you begin to converse about your life. After a while, Jesus asks you, "Where do you need healing in your life?" Take some time to respond to Jesus. Then you may sense Jesus asking another question: "Would you like me to touch you in a healing way?" How do you respond to that? If you are uncomfortable with touch, you may suggest an alternative way of healing. If you welcome Jesus' healing touch, imagine Jesus touching you. What do you feel? How does this transform your life?

Conclude your meditation with gratitude for God's healing touch in your life.

LIVING ADVENTUROUSLY

The right kind of touch can heal and transform. Today's exercise of experiencing healing touch may actually take months to achieve. You may need to research resources in your community. The first aspect of today's practice is to learn to receive healing touch. Take time to receive God's healing touch through the caring touch of another person who is trained in a healing practice such as massage, Reiki, or another hands-on modality. Explore receiving physical and spiritual care and affirmation from another. Let touch open you to the beauty of your body. (If you have previously experienced violent, abusive, or inappropriate touch, you may choose to seek out a skilled practitioner who is trauma-sensitive.)

The second aspect of this day's practice involves learning a gentle practice of healing touch. I invite you to learn Reiki, therapeutic touch, massage, or another type of healing touch for your own self-care and support of others. In most metropolitan areas, you can receive referrals from accredited massage schools. In touching yourself in healing ways, such as through self-massage and self-Reiki, you promote your own wellness and practice healthy self-love. In learning healing touch practices, you also may find yourself available to support others' well-being in loving, welcome, and safe ways.

The third aspect of this day's practice is to explore how you can initiate or support a congregational health or healing ministry in your faith community. This may involve participating in a Stephen Ministry training or another congregational care program, helping with a congregational healing service, visiting persons in the hospital or in their homes, or working with your church to advocate for health-care reform.

DAY 32

The Gift of Peace amid the Stresses of Life

He woke up and rebuked the wind, and said to the sea, "Peace! Be still!" Then the wind ceased, and there was a dead calm. He said to them, "Why are you afraid? Have you still no faith?"
—Mark 4:39-40

Stress is one of the greatest threats to personal and spiritual well-being. It is both destructive and addictive in nature. Physicians report that more than 75 percent of patient visits are related to the negative impact of stress on persons' overall health. Prolonged stress breaks down the immune system, taxes the cardiovascular system, disturbs the digestive system, and threatens our emotional and spiritual well-being. Yet, in almost any gathering of professionals, participants vie with one another to describe the stress they experience in balancing work and family. In many circles, the more stressful you describe your life, the more committed your colleagues assume you are to your work. Peace of mind and equanimity are often viewed as signs of lack of commitment and ambition.

Jesus the Healer called persons to abundant life. For Jesus, fullness of life involved the integration of adventure, challenge, risk taking, and hard work. Jesus spent long days teaching, preaching, and healing. He also regularly sought peace in quiet places. As a model for today's professionals, Jesus' ministry balanced hard work with sabbath rest.

Stress can contribute to growth as well as disease. Physicians and counselors speak of "good stress" and "bad stress." Good stress involves the challenges we experience in any significant change, whether chosen or unexpected—beginning an exercise regimen, going back to school, exploring new gifts and talents, falling in love, or facing our fears. Bad stress involves the anxiety that arises from having too much to do in too little time, from making too many commitments, from trying to please people, or from seeing the world in terms of competition and opposition rather than interdependence and partnership. This is especially true of professional caregivers, such as social workers, nurses, physicians, and ministers. Over time, negative stress may lead to distress, burnout, and physical disease.

Stress and distress are often a matter of perspective and faith. The biblical tradition challenges us to find sabbath time amid the demands of our busy and challenging lives. Psalm 46 describes a time of personal and national tumult and then counsels the faithful community to "Be still, and know that I am God!" (v. 10). We can find a quiet center even in the most distressing times.

The Gospel of Mark tells the story of a storm at sea (4:35-41). Buffeted by the waves, the disciples were panicking until they realized that Jesus was with them in the boat. As I visualize the story, at the moment they called upon Jesus, the disciples experienced a sense of peace, even though the storm was still raging. I find two miracles within the story. The first miraculous event is the healing of perspective that occurred when the disciples realized that Jesus was their companion in the storm. Whatever happened, they realized that they would be safe. Second, Jesus calmed the storm with a word of peace. Jesus first calmed the disciples' inner life and, in that peaceful moment, the external world was transformed.

Living adventurously often places us in stress-filled situations. You may have to work long hours for periods of time in order to achieve excellence in living out your vocation. You may have to challenge authority figures about inappropriate decisions or unjust practices. You may have to balance excellence in your work with care for a sick child or an aging relative. You will undoubtedly have to explore new behaviors and take the road less traveled. But, in all these situations, you can experience peace one moment at a time—first by remembering that God is our partner in our adventures, and then by committing yourself to regular spiritual practices that calm the spirit and enlarge the heart. In that calming moment, you will experience the reality of the "relaxation response," described by physician Herbert Benson.[4] Simply by closing your eyes and focusing without judgment on a meditative word, you can experience spiritual and physiological well-being. The relaxation response reveals the deep truth that peace is only a moment away when you awaken to God's ever-present care. With God as your companion, you always have enough time and energy to live abundantly and justly, even in challenging times.

A Prayer for the Adventure

Loving God, amid the storms of life, calm my soul. Remind me that you are always with me, and that in your presence, I cannot fail. With your grace, I will remain calm amid stress and conflict. In the stillness, let me hear your voice and know that I am safe. In my safety, let me bring your calm to others. In Christ's name. Amen.

CHOOSING YOUR OWN AFFIRMATION

Knowing that stress and distress are a matter of perspective, your use of affirmations awakens you to a larger world in which you have everything you need to serve God and live with abundance. Take time throughout the day to repeat these peaceful affirmations, especially when you feel your stress level increasing.

- God is with me in all the storms of life.
- I experience peace in every situation.
- Peace is only a moment away.
- I experience peace in (*a particular situation*).

Your Holy Imagination

In this imaginative prayer, you will discover Jesus' presence in the storms of life.[5] Take time to quietly and meditatively read the story of the storm at sea (Mark 4:35-41). Then become part of the scene. It is a glorious day, and you are about to sail across a lovely lake. Imagine the lake—the color of the waters, the environment, and the sailboat. Feel the gentle breeze as you set sail.

Today you are celebrating with friends. Who is traveling with you? What food and drink do you take with you? You have also invited Jesus the Savior and healer to join you. Take a moment to imagine Jesus—what does he look like? What does he bring for the "potluck" celebration? Visualize yourself and your companions gently sailing across the sea, soaking in the beauty of the place, as you tack with the winds.

Suddenly a storm comes up. The skies darken, waves crash against the boat, lightning flashes, and thunder booms. Your sailboat is tossed around like a small toy. You and your companions work feverishly to keep the sailboat from capsizing. How do you feel with the storm raging all around?

Looking at your life today, what storms are raging? How are they shaping your life? What are your feelings about them? Do you feel stress or helplessness, or some sense of control?

In the midst of the storm, you remember that Jesus is with you in the boat. How do you feel when you remember that Jesus is with you? Jesus awakens and simply says, "Peace." The storm suddenly ceases. The sky clears. You sail home on a gentle sea.

Conclude this meditation by thanking God for God's constant care and presence in your life.

Living Adventurously

Today's adventure will take you to "inner space." Take a few moments to experience the relaxation response through the ancient Christian practice of centering prayer.

Be still in God's presence. Take a deep, cleansing breath, letting go of any distress and focusing on your whole being. Feel your quiet spiritual center.

In centering prayer, you simply focus on a prayer word—such as *peace, joy, light, Christ, holy*, or *love*. Let the word gently well up in your being, and repeat it over and over for fifteen to twenty minutes. If your mind wanders, bring your consciousness back to the prayer word, without judgment. You may experience peace without words in the course of your prayer.[6]

During the day, whenever you begin to experience stress, simply take a moment to breathe deeply and silently invoke your prayer word. Studies indicate that centering prayer and the relaxation response calm body, mind, and spirit. Persons who regularly practice centering prayer experience deep physiological well-being simply by invoking their prayer word in a time of stress. Through the use of spiritual practices, we are always only a moment away from peace of mind.

DAY 33

Finding God in the Darkness

Where can I go from your spirit? . . . If I ascend to heaven, you are there;
   if I make my bed in Sheol, you are there. . . .
If I say, "Surely the darkness shall cover me,
   and the light around me become night,"
even the darkness is not dark to you,
   the night is as bright as the day,
   for darkness is as light to you.

—Psalm 139:7-8, 11-12

God's holy adventure embraces darkness as well as light. Personal healing and wholeness must include both prevention and response to health challenges if it is truly to respond to the well-being of the whole person. In the preface to Margaret Guenther's *Holy Listening*, Alan Jones notes that spirituality deals with the "unfixable" aspects of our lives.[7] His words remind us that darkness also has a light of its own. Within the darkness, the seedling grows. Within the womb, new life takes form. Within the chrysalis, the caterpillar transforms into a butterfly. Still, we often fear the dark and flee from the unfixable aspects of life that will eventually be our companions on our own holy adventure.

I must admit that I love darkness. I feel a special sense of peace on an early morning walk, and I experience holy wonder in stargazing during the wee hours of the morning. But unexpected sounds in the dark may startle me and put me on "high alert" both in attention and physiology. I have noticed that we can be lost in the darkness, but we can also find wholeness within life's darkest, fear-filled moments. Just a glimmer of light can pierce the deepest darkness.

The mystic/theologian/pastor Howard Thurman reminds us that when we attend to the divine light within our lives and the world, we can find our way through the deepest darkness. The story is told of one hot summer day when young Thurman went berry picking. He plunged deeper and deeper into the woods behind his grandmother's house, picking and eating the ripe juicy berries, until his happy adventure was interrupted by a flash of lightning and the crash of thunder in the distance. Suddenly, as the sky grew dark, he realized he was lost. Deep within the woods, he could see nothing familiar. Panicked, he was tempted to start running, even though he had no idea which way to go. At that moment, he remembered something his grandmother had told him: "If you don't know what to do, just stop awhile and look around." So he stopped and waited and looked—in all four directions—as lightning flashes illumined the woods. Finally he saw something vaguely familiar and decided to walk toward it. Proceeding very slowly, he was able to get his bearings with each lightning flash until he found his way home. The same storm that frightened him also provided guidance toward home.

Psalm 139 describes the reality that if God is truly with us wherever we go, we are always "at home," even when we don't know it. Wherever we are, even when we are running away from God, we are, nevertheless, in God's loving arms. Despite our apparent distance from God, God never leaves us. As theologian Nelle Morton notes, "The journey is home!"[8]

The psalmist says in verse 11, "If I say, 'Surely the darkness shall cover me, and the light around me become night,' even the darkness is not dark to you; the night is as bright as the day, for darkness is as light to you." Anxiety, depression, and fear may dim our experience of God. But even when our inner struggles threaten our well-being, a divine light can still illumine our path. This light may come through the love of a listening friend, the help of a sensitive and gifted therapist, the support of a faithful community, or even a wisely prescribed medication. God always makes a way when there seems to be no way!

Our own emotional distress cannot banish God's deep presence and care for us. Guilt and shame cannot thwart God's everlasting love. Sadly, the lectionary and many responsive prayers neglect the words of anger and lament found in Psalm 139:19-22. Can you imagine saying, "O that you would kill the wicked, O God!" or "I hate them with perfect hatred," in private or in church? Most of us would feel guilty for even *thinking* such thoughts. But God accepts the totality of our lives and invites us to do likewise. I remember, in the moments following the terrorist attacks on 9/11, hearing a colleague of mine, a pacifist by nature, exclaiming, "Why don't we just nuke them all!" Strong language from the psalmist and a university professor! But even our anger, hatred, and guilt are an essential part of our prayer lives if we are to be truthful to ourselves and God.

Immediately after spewing words of hatred, the psalmist continues, "Search me, O God, and know my heart; test me and know my thoughts. See if there is any wicked way in me, and lead me in the way everlasting" (vv. 23-24). God will not stop loving us even if we no longer love ourselves. God will not hate us even when we hate others. Though our thoughts and actions influence how God works in our lives, the infinitely flexible God presents us with new possibilities and pathways for healing, wholeness, and self-awareness. In the darkest night, God's light shines, always showing us the way back home to ourselves and the path of holy adventure.

A Prayer for the Adventure

In darkness, O God, we experience your light shining upon us. Help me embrace light and dark, action and rest, birth and death. Help me accept my "shadow side" as a womb of possibility rather than shame. Help me take my whole life to you—joy and sorrow, friendship and anger, intimacy and alienation—knowing that you bless and heal all things by your love. Amen.

CHOOSING YOUR OWN AFFIRMATION

Affirmations are searchlights that illumine our spiritual path even on the darkest days. They focus on truths about God that we might otherwise overlook, and they help us find our way when we feel most spiritually and emotionally lost. Repeat one or more of these affirmations:

- Wherever I go, I am in God's hands.
- Regardless of how I feel, God supports me.
- Regardless of my thoughts and actions, God works to heal and guide me.
- I am always at home, because God is always with me.
- (*In a particular situation*), I am in God's supportive hands.

YOUR HOLY IMAGINATION

In this imaginative prayer, read Psalm 139:19-24. Let the words sink into the marrow of your being. Take a moment to examine your life. Who do you hate with a "perfect hatred"? Who would you like to see annihilated?

Take a moment to picture these persons' faces, and notice the feelings that emerge. Then, without letting go of your anger, visualize these people as beloved by God. Place them in God's care, and let God help you discern an appropriate response to such persons.

In the quiet, reflect on your own anger and hatred. What might be its deepest meaning? Toward what actions does it call you as a partner in

God's quest for justice? How can you mobilize your anger in ways that help you claim your vocation as an agent of divine justice and reconciliation?

Some Old Testament scholars see the psalms of anger and lament as reflections of the Hebraic community's response to injustice.[9] God's passion for justice was often experienced as divine anger directed toward those who treated the poor or vulnerable unjustly. Our anger may be a righteous part of God's quest for social justice. It is not to be eliminated but creatively framed in the context of our own humble confession of sin and our desire for God's shalom, the peace that embraces both the oppressed and oppressor.

> God's passion for justice was often experienced as divine anger directed toward those who treated the poor or vulnerable unjustly. Our anger may be a righteous part of God's quest for social justice.

LIVING ADVENTUROUSLY

Remind yourself throughout this day, regardless of your negative feelings and the challenging events of your life, that you are in God's hands. If you feel perplexed or overwhelmed, take time to be still and listen imaginatively for divine guidance. Make it a practice throughout the day to ask for clarity in your intuition of God's possibilities for justice and love, even when you do not feel anxiety or fear. Awakening to the divine light in all settings is a faithful discipline of the imagination and intuition that reminds you that you are always on holy ground. Follow divine guidance in your relationships throughout this day as you seek to speak words of justice and reconciliation.

DAY 34

We Experience God's
Strength in Our Weakness

My grace is sufficient for you, for power is made perfect in weakness.
—2 Corinthians 12:9

he late M. Scott Peck began his book *The Road Less Traveled* with the words "Life is difficult." God's holy adventure is also difficult. In the intricate interdependence of life, much of what happens to us is beyond our control. As Jesus said to the apostle Peter, "When you were younger, you used to fasten your own belt and to go wherever you wished. But when you grow old, you will stretch out your hands, and someone else will fasten a belt around you and take you where you do not wish to go" (John 21:18).

In describing his own holy adventure in 2 Corinthians 11:16–12:10, the apostle Paul spoke of a life filled not only with persecution and pain but also with grace and wonder. The same is true of our lives. Writing to the Christians in Corinth, Paul confessed that he was struggling with his own "thorn in the flesh," an unknown malady that diminished his overall quality of life. Despite his ardent prayers, vigorous Christian leadership, and mystical experiences, Paul's chronic illness remained unabated. While I do not attribute this ailment exclusively to divine activity, as Paul suggested, I believe that God's aim for wholeness in our lives embraces our vulnerability and pain as well as our success and joy. Growing in wisdom and stature involves accepting the totality of your life, both what you can change and what you must endure, as an opportunity to experience God's holy adventure more fully. The wisdom of the Cross is that God is as present in pain as in celebration.

C. S. Lewis rightly noted that the great religions of the world emerged in an era before the invention of pain relievers. Those who venture forth as partners in God's holy adventure will know great joy and great pain. We will experience empathetic pain as we attend to the cries of the poor, the despair of the abused, and the agony of the dying. Our pain will also be personal as we attend to our own quest for relational, psychological, or spiritual wholeness. We cannot hide from our pain and the pain of others if we seek to be God's partners in healing the world. If we live long enough, we will have our own personal struggles with aging, sickness, and dying. While we will prize independence, we will also learn the gift of vulnerability and interdependence. As he faced a life of pain and limitation, Paul also experienced a healing of the spirit, despite the fact that he was never cured. "My grace is sufficient for you, for power is made perfect in weakness," whispered God's voice (2 Cor. 12:9). Paul's confidence lay not in his own power but in the intricate interdependence of the universe, the Christian community, and the ever-giving God.

Left to ourselves, we are lost. But when we claim our place in God's dynamic and interdependent universe, we continually discover resources and inspiration beyond our own powers. This is a matter of trust in God and in others when we are least able to care for ourselves. Facing the prospect of Alzheimer's disease, pastor Robert Davis affirmed, "Many Christians have found that when life completely tumbles in, when they are without strength or any hope or help for themselves, or when their minds become too tangled to even hold thoughts, God overrules the circumstances and . . . comes to minister to them at the very point of their need."[10] When we open ourselves to God's cosmic adventure, God and those we love will supply our deepest needs in living and dying. Though we may wish to remain independent agents, we will become stronger in faith and life as we claim life's radical interdependence as a grace and a gift. With Robert Davis, we will experience divine wholeness as "a care receiver instead of a care giver."[11]

A Prayer for the Adventure

God of all seasons, we bring you our health and illness, our joy and our pain. Work within our vulnerability so that we might find your grace always sufficient for every need. Bless us with the spirit of inter-dependence, receiving and giving your grace in every encounter, accepting the love and help of others, even as we reach out to give help to others. Help us to experience holy vulnerability and compas-sionate care. In the name of the Healer, Jesus. Amen.

CHOOSING YOUR OWN AFFIRMATION

Spiritual affirmations testify to God's faithfulness when our own faith is weak. In repeating affirmative prayers, we discover the profound and holy interconnectedness that sustains us in each moment, especially when we reach the end of our independence and must trust the grace of God work-ing through our friends, family, and strangers. Try repeating the following affirmations and see what happens:

- God's grace is sufficient for me.
- I rejoice in the graceful interdependence of life.
- God strengthens me in my vulnerability.
- God's grace is sufficient for me in (*a particular life situation*).
- God strengthens me in (*a situation in which I am vulnerable and must depend upon others for my well-being*).

YOUR HOLY IMAGINATION

In this imaginative prayer, reflect on the graceful interconnectedness of life from the point of your greatest vulnerability. Breathe gently, inhaling the sheer goodness of life and the abundance of the universe. As you inhale, sense the nurturing presence of God and the universe that surrounds you. Breathe in the gifts of friends and loved ones as you picture them in your imagination. Breathe out your love for your friends and loved ones.

Breathe in, as you imagine them, the gifts of all who might support you throughout the day. Breathe out your gratitude for the many persons who anonymously support your life through the interdependence of economic systems—people like workers in canning factories, dairy farmers, and truck drivers.

In a similar spirit of interdependence, breathe in imaginatively the protective support of our national and local government and military leaders. Breathe out gratitude for your community's safety and social order that supports your personal freedom and creativity. Breathe in the support of our revolving planet and the universe beyond it. Breathe out the wonder of interconnectedness between the divine and all creation.

LIVING ADVENTUROUSLY

As you experience the profound interconnectedness of life, allow yourself to receive gifts and support of others in new ways. Accept generosity from others gratefully and graciously. Practice receptivity by experiencing what it is like to be on the receiving end of life. Today, give thanks to God and others for the many sources of your well-being. Express your gratitude as you receive the many gifts of others throughout the day.

DAY 35

We May Forget Ourselves, but God Will Never Forget Us

Can a woman forget her nursing child,
  or show no compassion for the child of her womb?
Even these may forget,
  yet I will not forget you.
See, I have inscribed you on the palms of my hands.
                                        —Isaiah 49:15-16

Virtually every human achievement is ambiguous in nature. As a result of education, diet, sanitation, and medical technology, we live longer and healthier lives. But our longevity has led to the growing challenges of maintaining quality of life amid the proliferation of chronic illnesses such as Alzheimer's disease, cancer, diabetes, and cardiovascular and pulmonary diseases. Many persons fear becoming victims of the technology intended to sustain and support life. Words that were unknown to our grandparents—such as AIDS, ALS, and Alzheimer's disease—strike terror in our hearts as we imagine our helplessness, vulnerability, and self-forgetfulness.

In many ways, Alzheimer's disease embodies many of our deepest fears—the loss of memory, reason, speech, and self-awareness. In the evolving human adventure, God loves each unique personal story. Tragically, the progression of Alzheimer's disease eventually robs us of our self-awareness and ability to remember our own personal stories. We may forget who we are and who we have been in the course of our unique personal adventure.

Alzheimer's disease threatens our very personhood. Again, Robert Davis portrays his own journey as well as the journeys of others with Alzheimer's disease: "In Alzheimer's disease there is the loss of the personality, a diminished sense of self-worth. A highly productive person has to wonder why he is still alive and what purpose the Lord has in keeping him on this earth. As I struggle with the indignities that accompany daily living, I am losing my sense of humanity and self-worth."[12] Yet, amid our fears of vulnerability and loss of self, we are called to remember that our value as God's beloved children is not based on reason, productivity, language, imagination, or even self-awareness, but on God's abiding, adventurous, and nonnegotiable love for all creation.

I believe that in the evolving adventure of living and dying, God never forgets us, nor does God quit working in our lives. All things are treasured in the divine memory. As the one to whom all hearts are open and all desires are known, God experiences each moment from the inside as well as from the perspective of its external relationships, and that includes persons with Alzheimer's disease, cancer, AIDS, and ALS.

If God is truly omnipresent and omniactive, then God is also present within the experience of persons with Alzheimer's disease. While we cannot fully fathom the nature of God's presence at such times, I believe that we experience God in our "sighs too deep for words." God is loving and faithful, even when we can no longer remember who we are. As a pastor, I have observed a deeper self than meets the eye in persons with Alzheimer's disease as they take Communion or remember the words of the Lord's Prayer or "Amazing Grace." At such moments, we experience God's whisper in their unexpected words.

The biblical tradition affirms that our experience of God's saving love is as much a gift of the faith of others as of our own faith. The healings of the young girl in a coma, Lazarus, and the man lowered from the rooftop depended not only on these individuals' faith, but also on the interplay of the faith of others and God's loving presence, embodied in Jesus the Healer. At life's extremities, we can trust the faith of the community to believe on our behalf when we can no longer pray, sing, or remember the traditions of faith. Imagining the future that awaits him, Robert Davis anticipates a time when he will consciously forget God's presence in his life. At that moment, Davis confesses, "I must rely solely on those who love me to keep me close to the Father by their prayers, and to reassure me with songs and touch and simple words of Scripture."[13] But, more than this, we can trust that God's inner voice will reassure us when we have no voice of our own; God's wisdom will support us when we can no longer remember who we are!

God's enduring love and unfailing memory remind us that we can believe on behalf of others, and others can believe on behalf of us. We can heal them by our healing words and touch and by singing hymns of faith, and vice versa. With awareness that God never forgets, we can accept our own fears of debilitation and experience God's healing touch precisely when we are most fearful of what the future may bring.

A Prayer for the Adventure

Holy Companion, help me to experience your unfailing love in health and illness, in success and failure. Help me to listen for your presence in my inner voice, through unexpected moments of inspiration, and through the care of others. Help me know that you are always with me and that nothing can separate me from your love in Christ Jesus, our Savior and Healer. Amen.

Choosing Your Own Affirmation

During times of depression and self-doubt, Martin Luther is said to have scrawled on his writing table the affirmation "I was baptized." That affirmation reminded Luther that his relationship with God depended on the Holy One, not on his own faith or productivity. Affirmations ground our lives in a Love that is greater than ourselves. Our security in remembrance and forgetfulness depends on the love of One who will never forget.

- Regardless of my state of mind, God loves me.
- I am God's beloved child in every season of life.
- Regardless of (*a particular health condition*), God loves me.
- I am God's beloved child in (*a particular season of my life, present or anticipated*).

Your Holy Imagination

Perhaps you remember the poem "Footsteps." In the poem, the unknown author has a dream that involves questioning God's fidelity in life's most difficult times. The author cites the presence of only one set of footsteps on the beach as proof of God's absence in times of need. Then the author is startled when God responds by revealing that when there was only one set of footprints, those footprints belonged to God. In other words, God carried the person through those tough times.

In this imaginative prayer, think of a time when you experienced a great personal struggle. What was your greatest fear? Did you feel God's presence or guidance? If so, take a moment to ponder imaginatively how God sustained and protected you. Did God carry you? Visualize God's loving care for you.

Now imagine a future time in which you feel vulnerable. What is your greatest fear? What might it be like to face that fear? As you visualize that difficult situation, sense God's presence with you. Whom do you envision as God's partners in your life at this time? Visualize God working through them to help you face your greatest fear. Bathe your spirit in God's never-failing love as embodied in God's presence and in your companions.

Living Adventurously

You can prepare for times of vulnerability by facing your fears, reaching out to others, and living adventurously. You can plan for the challenges of life by gathering support networks, planning for your estate, and becoming aware of case managers who will serve as resources for you and your loved ones in times of vulnerability.

Persons with Alzheimer's disease and other debilitating illnesses are often forgotten long before they die. Ruled by our fears, we often avoid such persons. Adventurous living challenges us to embrace our own vulnerability and the vulnerability of others, secure in our identity as God's beloved children.

While we must always be sensitive to a person's state of mind and overall health, we can bring joy and a sense of connectedness to persons with Alzheimer's disease by singing and praying with them. Often they know the words of familiar hymns and the Lord's Prayer as well as persons with good memories. If it is welcome and appropriate, we may touch them in a healing way, sharing with them the deep-down interconnectedness that soothes and heals any disease of body, mind, and spirit.

WEEK
6

GOD'S NEVER-
ENDING ADVENTURE

Martin Luther once affirmed that "[the law says:] 'In the midst of life we are surrounded by death,'" but the gospel reverses this sentence: 'In the midst of death we are surrounded by life.'" Though we may attempt to deny the reality of aging and death by technological, surgical, and cosmetic interventions, the mortality rate still remains at 100 percent. When I taught at Georgetown University School of Medicine, I often told my students, "You know all of your patients are going to die, but hopefully not on your watch!" It often seems to come as a surprise to church groups when I announce that everyone Jesus cured eventually died. The universality of death led C. S. Lewis to wonder if Jesus did Lazarus any favors, since Lazarus had to die twice! The reality of aging, death, and dying falls into the realm of the "unfixables" that every spiritual adventurer must explore.

The Bible affirms that death is inevitable for all things, from peasants and kings to governments and galaxies. The process of creative transformation that lies at the heart of our personal, communal, and planetary adventures arises from the cyclical dance of creation and destruction—and then new creation. Based on what we know of astrophysics, we can assume that even from the death of our solar system, new and unimaginable worlds will emerge. God recycles!

Death and dying are pathways to adventure that most of us would just as soon bypass on the road to eternity. In the modern world, we fear the process of dying—the reality of pain, vulnerability, and lack of control—as much as we fear the reality of death. To embrace their life as a holy adventure means fully embracing death, dying, and vulnerability as core human experiences within a larger perspective—the promise that though our earthly lives may perish, we will live forevermore as God's companions in a never-ending journey within the community of God.

Divine creativity continually births universes, galaxies, planets, and persons and lovingly receives their adventures back into God's everlasting life at their physical journey's end. Adventurous spirituality overcomes the dualisms of mind and body, heaven and earth, and life and death. Our bodies and spirits are holy and loved by God, now and forevermore.

The image of resurrection reminds us that God's everlasting life embraces, treasures, and transforms all that is good in this life within our ongoing postmortem adventures—embodiment, creativity, relationship, novelty. What happens in this lifetime is treasured in God's memory eternally and contributes to the everlasting journeys of ourselves and our companions.

All things share in eternity and therefore deserve our honor and care. What happens in this world truly matters in the here and now, both on its own terms and because it matters eternally to God. God never "loses" anything of value that occurs in this world. God forgets neither the fall of the sparrow nor your struggle with a life-threatening illness, painful childhood, or the loss of a beloved friend or spouse. Our adventures toward wholeness continue beyond the grave. What happens here on earth becomes part of our "eternal adventure."

Issues of ethics and justice are important, first of all, because of their impact on the lives of persons and communities in the here and now. Economic justice shapes the vision of possibilities and the overall health of God's beloved children in this lifetime. These same conditions shape our personalities and become the essential materials that are transformed and brought to wholeness in God's loving and everlasting community. Believe it or not, what we do today contributes to the eternal adventures of our planetary companions.

For many persons, the vision of eternal life can be threatening as well as reassuring. Dualistic images of the afterlife suggest a separation of the sheep from the goats and the saved and from the unsaved. In this dualistically divided universe, only certain humans can achieve their purpose in this life and the next. Others are not only lost eternally but also are condemned to utter darkness and meaninglessness. Such dualistic theology suggests that death is stronger than God! According to such a view, at the hour of death, God is rendered powerless—a victim, if you will, of God's own abstract justice, which ultimately proves itself stronger than God's love for creation. Stated another way, such dualistic theology asserts that God's attitude toward you immediately changes at the moment of your death. Though eternity lies ahead for you, if you have not chosen Christ as your Savior in the right way, your fate is sealed, and there is nothing God will or can do about it. From this perspective, God's love is finite, limited, and conditional.

In contrast, an adventurous and holistic spirituality affirms that God's never-ending holy adventure is dynamic and life-transforming. Creativity, relationship, and transformation continue beyond the grave. At death, God welcomes all things into an everlasting community of love and healing with the promise that unexpected adventures of growth and creativity lie ahead. Within God's realm both sheep and goats find a home.

The reality of God's all-embracing love defies dualisms of heaven and earth and saved and unsaved, reminding us that salvation is never a private or individual issue. Instead of a linear choice on our part, our openness to God's holy adventure is shaped by many factors. Often our ability to trust God is limited by genetics, chemical balance, family of origin, and the religious ideas we heard as children. Victims of various forms of abuse by spiritual leaders may never be able fully to trust God or their neighbors until they are bathed in a Love that has neither beginning nor end.

In the concreteness of our lives, there are no absolute boundaries between the faithful and the godless, or the saved and the damned. Saints protest their distance from divine perfection, and sinners transform their lives by unexpected acts of mercy. As a wise teacher once said, "There are only two kinds of people in the world: those who are in God's hands and know it, and those who are in God's hands and do not [yet] know it!" The key word is *yet*. In the spirit of Luke 15, God will not forsake any lost sheep until it is found, whether that means a lifetime or an eternity.

We are on a never-ending journey of grace and adventure in which time and eternity are radically open. The omnipresent and omniactive God will touch all of our hearts in such a way that our holy adventures and God's holy adventure for the cosmos will eventually evolve together in the great adventure of everlasting love and life. With God as our everlasting companion, we will discover that even in the midst of death, we are surrounded by life in all its beauty, love, and abundance!

DAY 36

God's Love Embraces This World and the Next

This is eternal life, that they may know you, the only true God, and Jesus Christ whom you have sent.

—John 17:3

"This is my Father's world, and to my listening ears all nature sings and round me rings the music of the spheres."[1] Adventurous spirituality proclaims God's lively presence in all things in this world and the next. Every place can be a "thin place" where God is revealed in the tasks of ordinary life. Every landscape can reveal a "ladder of angels" (Gen. 28:12), reminding us that God is wherever we are, even when we are most oblivious of God's presence. When Jesus prayed for God's reign to come "on earth as it is in heaven," he affirmed that everyone can experience God's presence as his or her deepest reality. We can experience eternal life right now in knowing God's love as the transcendent and immanent force giving life to all things.

All life is interconnected; that includes the relationship between heaven and earth. This relationship is not one of timelessness and temporality, perfection and imperfection, and better and worse, but one of divine revelation and creaturely receptivity. Our image of heaven expresses our hope that God will transform our lives within an environment where grace and growth are constant companions in an adventure toward wholeness for all things. God's loving community embraces this world and its achievements, preserving everything that is of value as the basis for our continuing spiritual evolution in the "next world," whatever and wherever that may be.

An adventurous spirituality, grounded in the recognition of the significance of this lifetime in our spiritual journeys, affirms that we are creating one another's eternity by what we do today. Our values, achievements, and acts of loving-kindness shape our identity and experiences in this world and beyond the grave. We seek justice in this lifetime because it promotes other persons' health, well-being, and spiritual growth now and in our future as members of God's loving community. At the moment of our death, our personal identities are not lost but cherished in an adventurous community in which God's presence and passion for wholeness is unfettered. In this loving community, the "lived omnipresence," which only occasionally characterizes our everyday experience, will become our daily delight.

God loves the world—this world in which "the birds their carols raise, the morning light, the flowers bright, declare their Maker's praise"—as well as any other worlds we can imagine. In the cosmic ecology of God's love, we don't have to wait until we die to experience the wonders of the "heavenly" realm. In this lifetime, what a joy it is to be God's fellow adventurers in bringing beauty and novelty to this good earth. As that childhood hymn concludes, with lines appropriate to our recognition of the fragility of the ecosphere, "God trusts us with this world, to keep it clean and fair. All earth and trees, the skies and seas, God's creatures everywhere."[2]

A Prayer for the Adventure

Loving Creator—Artist of galaxies, planets, and worlds to come—help us to trust your love for this world and this life. Help us to create beauty that endures as we celebrate the passing moment. Help us to see holiness in all things and glimpse your everlasting life in this world's most unlikely places. Amen.

CHOOSING YOUR OWN AFFIRMATION

Holy affirmations help us awaken us to a truly adventurous Christian worldview. Affirmations remind us that both this lifetime and the next are precious in God's sight.

- God loves this world and all that is in it.
- My life is an eternal gift to God.
- My loving actions bring joy to (*a particular person*) in this life and the next.
- I rejoice with God in the beauty of the earth.
- I rejoice with God in the beauty of (*a particular person or place*).

YOUR HOLY IMAGINATION

In this section, we will take time to reflect on life after death. While the afterlife remains a mystery even to those who have had near-death experiences, well-considered images of survival after death can give us inspiration and hope for the challenges of this lifetime.

Imagine your dying day. As you take your last breath, envision yourself entering the afterlife. What do you see? Do you see anyone familiar as you enter the next world? How do these persons relate to you? As you adjust to your new environment, what do you experience?

During your adventure in "the beyond," see yourself encountering a "being of light," perhaps even Jesus. What does this being say to you? Is there anything you want to ask this being of light? Imagine your conversation. As you talk about your lifetime, what feelings and thoughts do you notice? In light of your imagined heavenly destiny, what values are you challenged to embrace more fully in this lifetime?

Conclude by giving thanks and praise for the glorious adventure that you share with God and your earthly companions this day and in eternity. Remind yourself that *this* world shares in God's evolving love.

LIVING ADVENTUROUSLY

Today, commit yourself to living out your life in light of the creative inter-play of time and eternity. Commit yourself to experiencing each encounter as an eternal gift to God. Take time to treat everyone you meet as a beloved child of God, as your companion on an everlasting adventure throughout this life and the next. See yourself as contributing something beautiful to their eternal and holy adventure with God.

Remember that you are always on holy ground and that every place is a "thin" place where earthly time and everlasting life intersect.

DAY 37

Our Dying Can Be a Witness to God's Undying Love

[Nothing] will be able to separate us from the love of God in Christ Jesus our Lord.
—Romans 8:39

To believe that God's holy adventure embraces every aspect of life is to affirm that nothing can separate us from the love of God. Spiritual wholeness, integrity, and stature are tested in times of vulnera-bility and pain as well as success and ease. Marriages, intimate friendships, and personal vocations find their fulfillment in facing every season of life with fidelity and hope. Do you remember the traditional marriage vows?

> For better, for worse,
> For richer, for poorer,
> In sickness and in health.

It happens all the time. A young couple commits to a holy relationship with absolutely no idea of what will come. They make their vows with hope and trust that they will have the resources to respond to the unknown and the unexpected. We know that they will be tested in the course of their relational adventure. Deep down, they know this too and believe that over the next several decades, they will have the courage and fidelity to make the journey together.

For many of us, the confrontation with death and dying, either our own or that of a loved one, is the greatest challenge to our sense of a holy adventure. Simone de Beauvoir, in her account of her mother's death, noted that "the world had shrunk to the size of her [nursing home] room."[3] Even under the best of circumstances, the dying process and the experience of grief stretch our sense of self, faith in God, and ability to trust the mystery.

Death is truly a great adventure. While some have gained hope and solace from near-death experiences, life beyond the grave still remains a great mystery even to those who have encountered a "being of light." The interplay of life, death, and beyond is filled with unexpected twists and turns in which we may be called upon to let go of everything we love, face our limitations, and accept our vulnerability. We may have to depend on the kindness of strangers simply to go to the bathroom or eat our meals. We may have to let go of everything that previously defined our sense of self in order to embrace faithfully the new self we are becoming as we age or experience a chronic or terminal illness. In such moments, we may find that we do not even have the ability to make a conscious prayer. We may have to depend on others to sustain our faith. In the spirit of Jesus on the cross, we all will have to pray, "Father, into your hands I commend my spirit."

Today our holy adventure invites us to embrace a "new millennium" version of the medieval "arts of dying" through a commitment to prayer, contemplation, acceptance of vulnerability, and mindful living. When I was a medical school professor, I invited my students to view their own experiences of sickness and medical care as a way to empathize with their patients' experiences. Like them, we can prepare for our dying by "practicing" dying in response to situations of limitation and vulnerability. If we are currently able-bodied, we can experience rather than deny a wide range of feelings as we live with a minor illness or temporary physical limitation. We can learn to face what is beyond our control with equanimity. We can explore meditative prayers for peace of mind and relief of pain. Perhaps, most of all, we can prepare for our dying by living adventurously, lovingly, and mindfully. Despite our current health condition, each day can be an opportunity to proclaim, "This is the day that the LORD has made; let us rejoice and be glad in it" (Ps. 118:24). God is with you, sustaining and guiding you, as you face your greatest fears.

A Prayer for the Adventure

Everlasting Companion, I place my fear and anxiety about death and pain in your loving care. Hold my fears as you would a little child, reassuring me that I am not alone and that your love will be my companion in every season of living and dying. I place the past, present, and future in your care, trusting that you have a place for me in a realm that knows neither beginning nor ending nor death nor loss. In Christ's name. Amen.

CHOOSING YOUR OWN AFFIRMATION

Affirmations help us remember that God is with us, regardless of the situation. They witness to a reality that is deeper than pain and death. In so doing, they enable us to face what we cannot change with hope, courage, and conviction.

A friend of mine who runs marathons notes that somewhere around the twentieth mile, everything within him tells him it's time to quit. Although his muscles ache and his endurance ebbs, he keeps focused on the next six miles by affirming that he can do it—he has run the race before and will run this one as well.

Life is a marathon, not a race, and affirmations help us remember that we are not alone. We have the companionship of other adventurers, including God, when we pass through the darkest valley.

- Nothing can separate me from the love of God.

- God is present in my vulnerability.
- God gives me strength to face today's challenges.
- (*A particular situation of debilitation*) cannot separate me from the love of God.
- God is present in (*a situation of vulnerability*).

YOUR HOLY IMAGINATION

In this exercise, take a moment for quiet reflection. As you rest in God's peace, give yourself plenty of time to respond to these statements:
- When I reflect on my own death, I feel _____.
- When I think of my own death, my greatest fear is _____.
- I would like for _____ to be with me at my deathbed.

After reflecting on these statements, insofar as you are able, imagine yourself actually dying. Let yourself experience your greatest fear. What does it feel like emotionally? physically? spiritually?

In that moment of vulnerability, imagine yourself feeling the comfort of Christ with you. What do you say to Christ? What does he say to you?

As you lie in your bed, envision Christ lying beside you. See him crawling next to you and holding you in his loving arms. How does that feel? Look into Christ's eyes. Feel his everlasting love wrap around you.

Conclude by prayerfully affirming that you are always in God's hands. Thank God for the everlasting love that embraces you in living and dying.

LIVING ADVENTUROUSLY

Living adventurously involves both courageous thought and action. We must embrace the totality of our lives, including our fear and helplessness, as a means of encountering the deeper realities of God's love and our interconnectedness with all creation.

If you are living with a chronic illness or even facing a minor illness or physical or mental limitation, take time to examine your response to your illness or limitation. Try to experience your illness from a larger perspective that gives you a sense of peace, such as that suggested by the previous guided meditation. Reflect on your illness in light of the Serenity Prayer, noting what is and is not in your control. Be attentive to the "Christ moments" present in your illness or limitation, and also to your sense of vulnerability.

Giving and receiving are profoundly related. If you are able and have a sense of calling to do so, consider volunteering at a hospice. Take time to view the vulnerable residents at the hospice as God's beloved children in need of your care and support. As you see Christ in their lives, perhaps you can be Christ for them. Prayerfully experience the intricate intimacy of life that joins the living with the dying, and the healthy with the sick in God's ecology of relationships.

DAY 38

God Is Our Companion
on the Journey of Grief

Grieve as those who have hope.

—1 Thessalonians 4:13, AP

I n describing his response to the death of his wife, C. S. Lewis spoke of bereavement as being "like a long valley, a winding valley where any bend may reveal a totally new landscape."[4] As I mentioned yesterday, our journey of healing through death and bereavement begins when we recognize our own mortality and the mortality of those we love. The finality of death transforms our life and moves us along the pathway of our holy adventure in ways we can never imagine, breaking down our defenses and piercing our spirits. As Lewis noted, "I had my miseries, not hers; she had hers, not mine. The end of hers would be the coming-of-age of mine."[5]

Once again, I invite you to remember that our experience of grief is grounded in the holy interconnectedness of life. Those who allow themselves to be profoundly shaped by their relationships with others will always sense they have lost an essential part of themselves when they lose a beloved companion or friend. Painful as it may be, healthy grieving also recognizes itself as a celebration of relationship. The process of grief moves toward wholeness as we creatively let go and celebrate significant love relationships in our lives.

The story is told of a woman who came to Gautama Buddha, carrying the lifeless body of her child. Distraught with grief, she begged the spiritual teacher to restore her child to health. The Buddha told her that he would revive her child, provided she met one condition: she needed to bring him a mustard seed that came from a family that had never lost a parent, spouse, brother, sister, or beloved animal to death. Later that day the mother returned without a mustard seed but healed of her grief, for she had experienced the universality of loss and bereavement. While the healing process may not be that simple for most of us, it is clear that death and loss are essential and unavoidable aspects of the human adventure. Placing our own sorrow in the context of God's holy adventure, we can discover the pathway to healing and wholeness. To grieve is to have loved. In creatively and faithfully experiencing our grief, we may discover that the other side of grief is our gratitude for the depths of love we have felt for another.

When we grieve, we can catch a glimpse of what Rabbi Abraham Joshua Heschel described as the "divine pathos," the suffering of the Intimate Companion who loves us and all we love, and feels our pain as God's own. Jesus wept at the loss of his friend Lazarus and the pain that overwhelmed Mary and Martha. As German pastor, theologian, and martyr Dietrich Bonhoeffer asserted, "Only a suffering God can save."

We find healing and wholeness not by avoiding grief, but by embracing our pain in light of God's tender companionship embodied in our closest relationships. We must experience the shock, anger, depression, and brokenness of grief in order to find the healing that enables us to reach out to others again. In such moments of honesty and pain, we can discover, with the authors of the Psalms, that God's love is great enough to accept the totality of our lives, including our anger and pain.

Sadly, the experience of loss often brings out the worst examples of popular theology. C. S. Lewis confessed:

> Not that I am (I think) in much danger of ceasing to believe in God. The real danger is of coming to believe such dreadful things about Him. The conclusion I dread is not, "So there's no God after all," but, "So this is what God's really like. Deceive yourself no longer."[6]

In the days following the death of a loved one, well-meaning friends remind us that our beloved's death is "God's will," or that "God only takes the good ones," or "God never gives you a problem you can't handle." Often we feel guilty about the pain we have caused for another or about our failures as a friend, spouse, or parent. As I look at my own grief over the loss of both parents, I know that although I did my best to support and nurture them in their final years, I still could have been a more attentive and empathetic son. I could have been more understanding, self-revealing, and supportive, and I mourn countless opportunities to break down the barriers that stood between us. At such moments, we need to remember that God is "the fellow sufferer who understands," as philosopher Alfred North Whitehead asserts. God feels our pain, anguish, and guilt. God knows the good we failed to do and the pain we inflicted. God embraces our lives in their totality and calls us to experience healing in the midst of our pain.

We can grieve with hope because God is not finished with our lives or the lives of those we love. Despite our pain and doubt, we can trust that God has a vision of wholeness for us and our beloved. As we look toward the future without our loved ones, we can take comfort in God's caring words to the prophet Jeremiah, "For surely I know the plans I have for you . . . plans for your welfare and not for harm, to give you a future with hope" (29:11).[7]

A Prayer for the Adventure

God, who has loved us into life and whose love sustains us through all of life's changes: Help us to embrace the seasons of life, from birth to death, youth to old age, romance to bereavement, knowing that you are always with us. Open us to our pain as well as our joy with the awareness that by accepting our grief and pain, we can more readily accept the wholeness and joy that you have planned for us. Open us to healing opportunities when we encounter those who grieve. In the name of Jesus the Healer. Amen.

CHOOSING YOUR OWN AFFIRMATION

Affirmations are spiritual reminders that you are never alone and that, with God as your companion, you have all the resources you need to face the challenges of grief and loss.

- God is with me in my grief.
- I embrace my sorrow, knowing that God is with me.
- I can respond to (*a particular loss*) with God as my companion.
- God will guide me in responding to (*a particular loss*).

YOUR HOLY IMAGINATION

Your ability to respond to your own and others' bereavement in ways that promote healing is related to your response to previous experiences of grief. What remains hidden or unresolved in the past will often surface in future experiences of loss. Remembering your losses can be very painful. If you feel emotionally overwhelmed during today's process of reflection and imagination, seek the counsel of a therapist, a spiritual guide, or your pastor. If you have recently lost a loved one, you may choose simply to remember the other's life in thanksgiving rather than doing this exercise.

Return to a place and time where you experienced an important loss. What was the occasion? How did you feel at the time? How did others respond to the loss? How do you feel about the loss today?

What was the greatest joy you experienced in relationship to the one you lost? Take a moment to give thanks to God and celebrate your relationship with your loved one. Thank God for the gift of that relationship.

As you remember your loss, take a moment to imagine Christ with you. What would you like to share with Christ? Would you like Christ to touch you or hold you? In the midst of your grief, feel the warmth of Christ's loving touch and presence. Let the love of Christ heal the pain of any grief that remains with you today.

LIVING ADVENTUROUSLY

In a profoundly interdependent universe, "it takes a village" to help us creatively traverse every important life passage. Many persons have found healing through sharing their grief in bereavement support and spiritual healing groups. Such groups provide care, challenge, and consistency of friendship and enable us to experience the healing power of Christ through caring relationships.

> In a profoundly interdependent universe, "it takes a village" to help us creatively traverse every important life passage.

Investigate whether your community of faith has a professional or peer-led grief support group. If not, what resources are available within other faith communities in your area? If you feel called, perhaps you might research the possibility of starting a support group in your community of faith or in partnership with other faith communities.

If your congregation has a Stephen Ministry or a similar lay pastoral care program, consider whether or not you might be called to participate in such a ministry.

DAY 39

With God as Our Companion, We Embrace the Mystery

For now we see in a mirror, dimly, but then we will see face to face. Now I know only in part; then I will know fully, even as I have been fully known.

—1 Corinthians 13:12

There is more to ourselves and our lives than we can ever imagine. God is still creating. God's plans are new every morning. Each moment we receive only a glimpse of the possibilities awaiting us in each situation. As the source of holy adventure, God not only provides but also receives new possibilities in the ongoing evolution of the universe and each creature in it. God calls us to be holy adventurers as well, trusting what we don't know and being humble about what we do know.

"There is more" is the call to embrace the beauty and mystery all around us. Every day involves the exploration of uncharted realities. Even though millions have passed this way before, we are called to walk the path from birth to death with fresh eyes and a beginner's mind. Though we are connected to the whole universe, our path of life is unique and unrepeatable.

As Paul wrote in 1 Corinthians 13:12, "Now we see in a mirror, dimly." This verse not only describes the nature of love but also our relationship to the most important realities of life.

Our holy adventures involve the interplay of what mystics have called the *kataphatic* and *apophatic* ways. On the one hand, God's omnipresence invites us to experience God in all things and all things in God. This reality calls us to kataphatic, or image-filled, spiritual practices. Every moment is a holy moment, every place a shrine, every face an incarnation. On the other hand, God is more than we can imagine. God is the deep mystery that reminds us that all things are also mysterious at their depths. This ineffable mystery calls us to apophatic, or nonimagistic, spiritual practices, which involve silence and wordless contemplation. We can never fully fathom the mystery of the Siamese cat purring on our lap or the mystery of the vastness of outer space. Nor can we fully fathom our own unique adventure. Deep calls unto deep, and all things become "thous," transparently revealing the divine, yet hiding God in their utter singularity.[8] As holy adventurers, we affirm the spirit of the following chant:

Changeless and calm, Deep Mystery
Ever more deeply rooted in Thee.[9]

A sense of God's deep mystery provides the antidote for too much certainty about subjects such as the afterlife. Too much certainty perpetrates violence upon persons and belief systems alike. It can lead to exclusion, objectification, and spiritual abuse in faith communities; intellectual abuse in academics; and emotional abuse in relationships. When we think we have all truth, we create artificial boundaries between companions and outsiders, saved and unsaved, orthodoxy and heresy. Those outside our religious camp can become the objects of spiritual warfare and violence when we assert that to become one of "us," others must forsake their deepest insights and understandings of the holy and unconditionally accept ours. We may even threaten anyone who does not hold our views with the ultimate act of spiritual and ideological violence: eternal damnation and alienation from God.

The original texts of Mark's Gospel end with the story of the empty tomb (16:1-8). Unlike Matthew and Luke, Mark does not record explicit encounters with the risen Christ. This abbreviated ending feels unsatisfying to those seeking certainty about resurrection and eternal life. But for those who embrace God's mystery with excitement and creativity, the empty tomb becomes the gateway to an open future that calls to us. It is the womb from which new life bursts forth in life's most unexpected moments.

All we need to know is that Christ is "not there" in the tomb but has gone before us in this life and the next. In the deep mystery of life and death, Christ will provide a way toward the eventual destination of God's loving community.

A Prayer for the Adventure

When we seek too much certainty, O Mysterious Companion, remind us that faith embraces the unseen and the unknown. Help us to trust that your loving presence is sufficient for anything the future brings. Remind us that just as we born into your loving arms, we will die into your loving arms. As we trust your love always, help us be safe and strong companions for the grieving, the dying, and the doubting. May we help others find their faith in companionship with us one step at a time. Amen.

CHOOSING YOUR OWN AFFIRMATION

Affirmations illumine our path into God's mystery. By definition, affirmations present an alternative reality to our present experience, thereby leading us deeper into the mystery of our own lives and the vast possibilities that lie ahead in partnership with the One who calls us to adventure.

- I trust God with life's mysteries.
- I journey into the unknown with God as my companion and guide.
- I trust God with (*a particular life mystery*).
- I experience new birth in (*a time of change*).

YOUR HOLY IMAGINATION

In this imaginative prayer, we once again encounter Jesus the teacher and healer. During this quiet time, ponder the mysteries of life—and of your life in particular. What mysteries do you find most intriguing? What mysteries do you wrestle with the most? What questions invite you to deeper faith? What questions do you have for God about these mysteries? Take time simply to sit with these questions.

Imagine once again that you discover Jesus, or another spiritual figure, sitting beside you. Ask him some of your deepest questions. How does he respond? Does he tell you a story or simply smile in silence? What does he leave mysterious? How does he respond to your desire for answers?

As you converse with Jesus, feel a gentle, warm light envelop you and illuminate your ponderings. As he departs, hear Jesus promise: "I will be with you always as a light that warms and guides. My light will always guide your steps as you journey into the mystery of your life."

LIVING ADVENTUROUSLY

German poet Rainer Maria Rilke encourages us to love the questions that echo into the mystery. We are also invited to love the mystery itself, whether it is in ourselves, our loved ones, God, or our future.

Today, commit yourself to remaining open to the questions, the mystery, and the "more" that characterize all things. In every encounter, look deeper to see what might be there beyond your first glance. Peer into the deeper dimensions of a spouse or partner, child, friend, stranger, or even a companion animal. Cherish the mystery of this individual's unique beauty and wisdom, life and love.

During this day, whenever you become anxious about your own future or the future of your loved ones, pause for a moment, take a deep breath, and name your fear and anxiety as you place the future in God's care. God is already with you and will be with you in the future. By prayerfully opening yourself to the mystery that lies ahead of you, you will experience a sense of peace and presence that will strengthen and sustain you, enabling you to respond creatively to those you love.

DAY 40

Everything Is Wrapped in God's Eternal Embrace

Remember, I am with you always, to the end of the age.
—Matthew 28:20

For some Christians, faith is ultimately about heaven and how to get there. According to this view, while we may achieve God's purposes for our lives here on earth, what matters most is our eternal salvation. From this perspective, apart from an explicit and personal relationship to Jesus Christ, we are eternally lost, regardless of what we have achieved on earth.

It is no coincidence that the Greek word for salvation means "wholeness" and "health." I believe that God's holy adventure lovingly embraces both this world and the next. What we accomplish in this lifetime lives on eternally in God's memory, shaping our own and others' adventures not only in this life but also in the afterlife. This life—your life, my life, this moment—truly matters, not just as a stepping-stone to eternity or as a passing contribution to divine memory, but for your pure wonder and joy, and God's pure wonder and joy, at our being alive in this place and time. This is the day! And so is tomorrow, and so on into God's everlasting realm.

Jesus healed persons for abundant life in this world as well as in "the next." He rejoiced in the flight of sparrows, the beauty of lilies of the field, and the wonder of children. He encouraged us to believe that eternity will take care of itself if we live as fully as possible now, trusting that we are God's partners in honoring and nurturing beauty and justice.

We do not have to choose between heaven and earth. The joy of this life and the next is part of God's aim at abundance for all creation. Divine omnipresence encompasses both earth and heaven. While God has a personal and unique relationship to each moment of existence, God's attitude toward creation cannot be loving and supportive in one part of creation and wrathful and alienating in another part. God can't be just a little omnipresent or just a little all-loving! Divine love embraces all things at all times and in all places, without limit or condition. Our openness to God shapes what God can do in our lives. But even when we turn away from God, God is luring us toward our true home as companions in the never-ending holy adventure of love.

Recall the Old Testament story of Jonah. It is so much more than a fish story! God never gave up on this wayward prophet, even though he responded to God's call not just reluctantly but by going in the opposite direction. Despite Jonah's hatred of the citizens of Nineveh, God continued to pursue Jonah, inviting him to be an agent of salvation. At the end of the story, the reader is left wondering whether Jonah's adventure was really about the salvation of Nineveh or Jonah's own salvation. Perhaps it was about both, since in the dynamic interdependence of God's beloved community, as Martin Luther King Jr. discovered, I cannot achieve my personal wholeness unless you also achieve your personal wholeness.

Ultimately, the image of God's "wrath," so beloved in certain Christian circles, is not about divine destructiveness and violence but rather about God's opposition to all that stands in the way of justice and wholeness. Thus, there is no contradiction between the ideas of divine justice and universal salvation.

Divine justice involves looking at our lives and our communities from God's point of view in order to experience our deepest vocation and heal our relationships and the relationships of others with whom we travel along our life's journey. Divine justice asks, "What is it you plan to do with your one wild and precious life?"[10] God also asks, "How are you contributing to the beauty and well-being of the earth and its inhabitants? How well are you practicing justice, loving mercy, and hearing the cries of the poor?" If this life is a process of spiritual evolution and transformation, you can only imagine the beauty and wonder of God's loving community in which Christ will bring wholeness to all things.

In describing the mystery of resurrection, the apostle Paul proclaimed that Christ will bring healing and reconciliation to all creation, so that "God may be all in all" (1 Cor. 15:28). Every creature will experience its true relationship with God, and in that experience each will claim her or his vocation as God's beloved child.

The good news is not only that God loves you but also that God loves all things eternally. This is a gospel that we can and must share, not in order to rescue humankind from eternal damnation but so that we and others can more fully experience God's holy adventure in this lifetime and in the next. Again, the gospel of God's holy adventure proclaims that there are only two kinds of people in the world: those who are in God's hands and know it, and those who are in God's hands and do not yet know it. To know you are in God's hands forever is to awaken to a world of exciting possibilities and relationships. We can face tomorrow as God's partners in healing the world, with courage even when we are fearful, with boldness even when we are timid, and with imagination even when we are faced with serious limitations.

When we choose to believe that God's love embraces everyone, not just a chosen few, we want to treat everyone we meet as God's beloved, eternal child. God calls holy adventurers to reverence life in its entirety and give thanks for each day as part of a never-ending journey toward healing and wholeness. God challenges us to work for justice and peace, even if the success of our efforts is in doubt. We know that our efforts join God's efforts to create a world of beauty and love in which God will eventually be honored as the Source of new life and creative transformation.

A Prayer for the Adventure

God, whose everlasting love flows through all things and whose creativity has neither beginning or end, help me to trust your everlasting life in my swiftly passing life. Enable me to trust those I love to your love. Guide me to love this good earth as your beloved creation, knowing that both this life and the next reflect your love and vision for healing and wholeness. Empower me to boldly share my love, secure in your everlasting love and as your partner in the adventures of this life and the next. In Christ's name. Amen.

CHOOSING YOUR OWN AFFIRMATION

You can experience God's everlasting life today! You can embrace this world fully even as you live in the light of God's transformation of your life and of all things. The following affirmations can help you claim God's presence everywhere in this world and in the next.

- I am in God's hands this day and forevermore.
- (*A friend or relative*) is in God's hands this day and forevermore.
- God's love embraces all things eternally.

- God's love embraces all things eternally, even (*a difficult person or enemy of our nation*).

YOUR HOLY IMAGINATION

In this imaginative prayer, envisage what it means for God to be "all in all" and to be experienced in all things as the Source of love and creative transformation. Take a few moments simply to breathe in God's everlasting and transformative love. As you rejoice in God's love, feel God transforming your life right now, in this moment, and forevermore. How does it feel to imagine God's holy adventure as your deepest reality? Using your imagination, see yourself and your loved ones living out of God's fullness. What does it look like?

Now envision living out of God's fullness in some of your closest relationships. Imagine your faith community living out of the fullness of God's loving community. What might it look like to imagine your nation, then the planet, with its human and nonhuman citizens, living within God's loving community? Imagine that loving community stretching out into eternity. Experience your life as lovingly connected with all things, giving and receiving God's universal love throughout time and eternity.

Conclude with a moment of gratitude for God's abundant love and resourcefulness in your life and in all things, and for your ability to imagine your life and the world in new and creative ways.

LIVING ADVENTUROUSLY

Throughout the day, in tasks large and small, remember your role in healing the universe. In each encounter, commit yourself to acting as a partner with Christ in bringing about a world in which "God may be all in all." Claim each encounter as an opportunity to humbly experience God's aim for your life and the universe. Do your best to trust your life to God's infinite love, and treat each person you meet as God's beloved child who shares in that same infinite love.

DAY 41

The Adventure Continues

Then Jesus said [to the women at the tomb], "Do not be afraid; go
and tell my brothers to go to Galilee; there they will see me."
—Matthew 28:10

oyful anticipation amid great mystery characterizes the holy adventure at every step. This applies not only to this lifetime but also to
life after death. Now we see in a mirror dimly, often hoping for enough illu-
mination for our next step. Yet we need not despair, because we can trust
in God's resourcefulness, fidelity, and inspiration. We don't need to know
everything about ourselves, others, or God's vision of the future to be able
to live joyfully and hopefully today. The God who will be "all in all" will
guide us as we journey into the future!

In speaking of God's nature, the North African theologian Augustine
once asserted that if you think you know it, it isn't God, but a finite object.
We can rejoice that God is always more than we can imagine. God's holy
adventure in all its dimensions calls us to develop our imaginations and
open ourselves to God through our imagination more and more every day.

Recognizing the limitations of our imaginative experience of God's
vision for the future is, ironically, the source of our hope rather than our
despair. When our vision diminishes and our resources fail, we can trust that
there is One whose love, inventiveness, and fidelity are beyond our wildest
imaginings. We can trust God's future precisely because "there is more."

Reports of near-death experiences describe a community of love and
light characterized by growth, interdependence, and companionship with
God and those we have loved.[11] Studies suggest that death is not the end of
a journey but a passage toward new and more wondrous adventures in
companionship with God and those we have loved. The darkness we imagine when we face the unknown is pregnant, as Psalm 139 proclaims, with
the everlasting light of God.

Words such as *eternal life* and *resurrection* express the reality that although we will die, "there is more" than we can ever imagine to ourselves, those we love, and to God's holy adventure. We do not know if our passage at the moment of death to the afterlife adventure will be abrupt or gradual, but to affirm that there is an afterlife is a statement of faith that what is good about this lifetime will be embraced and transformed in some mysterious way in the world to come.

Christian hope affirms that God will be "all in all." God will complete the good work that God began in your life and in the world. The new creation is birthed by transformation, not annihilation. Annihilation is not the way of God. In God's holy adventure, "no child is left behind!" God creates and embraces life in all its personal, cultural, and religious diversity in this life and the next.

The Revelation to John places images of destruction in the context of God's redemption of all things.[12] Yes, we may experience the pain of recognizing how often we failed to see God in our lives and in the world, and, yes, our sins of commission and omission will "follow" us as God's quest for justice and truth calls us to review our lives. However, I believe that we will also see the beauty that has been in our lives and in the lives of those we have loved. I believe we will also glimpse the beauty God intends for us in God's never-ending cosmic adventure. This is the spirit of Christian hope found in Revelation 21:3-5:

> See, the home of God is among mortals.
> He will dwell with them as their God;
> they will be his peoples,
> and God himself will be with them;
> he will wipe every tear from their eyes.
> Death will be no more;
> mourning and crying and pain will be no more. . . .
> See, I am making all things new.

How would you live your life if you truly believed that you couldn't lose? What if you believed that the same God who loved you into life and guides you even now as you read this book, also promises you everlasting life at the end of the adventure of this lifetime? I believe your life would be abundantly exciting and full of newness, love, and light!

As we conclude our sojourn together, I pray that you truly come to know that you are part of God's holy adventure. Your life is exciting because God has invited you to "choose your own adventure" and be God's companion in healing the world. This is the day God has made; this is the day of God's holy adventure. Let us rejoice and tell the world! God loves you and is at work in your life in bold, beautiful, and adventurous ways now and forevermore!

A Prayer for the Adventure

O Holy Adventure, from now on help me live each day adventurously, open to the surprises of each moment. Open my spirit to your spirit of new creation, trusting that all will be well in my life and in the lives of those I love. May your holy adventure inspire each day in its sheer wonder and giftedness. When I go to bed each night, let me trust the unknown to your care. Help me live each day in the certainty that every ending gives birth to a new beginning in the wondrous holy adventure that embraces life, death, and beyond. In the name of the resurrected and resurrecting Christ. Amen.

CHOOSING YOUR OWN AFFIRMATION

Affirmations remind us of God's story within each of our stories. The theme of that story is God's promise of salvation and wholeness throughout the many stories of our lives.

- I have an important role in God's everlasting adventure.
- I am God's beloved child, and I cannot lose in life's adventure.
- God has given me all the resources I need to be God's companion in healing the world.
- I am God's beloved child, and I cannot lose in (*a particular life situation*).

- God has given me all the resources I need to be God's companion in healing (*a particular life situation*).

YOUR HOLY IMAGINATION

Psalm 118:24 proclaims, "This is the day that the LORD has made; let us rejoice and be glad in it!" Think of that—this is the day! Salvation and wholeness are available right now. We live eternal life one moment at a time every day. Each moment is holy and provides an opportunity to be God's partner in healing our lives and the entire universe.

In today's exercise, take time to reflect deeply on what you will do as you come to believe that your life is in God's hands forever and that God's dream for your wholeness will never be thwarted by any circumstances in this life or the next.

Let your imagination play. Let it dance and spin out the most beautiful scenario that you can imagine. Imagine yourself proclaiming, "This is the day that God has made, and I will rejoice and be glad in it." What beauty will you bring to the world? What simple but beautiful adventures do you see yourself having? What do you see yourself doing for the pure joy of it, simply for fun with your fun-loving God as your companion in beauty and joy? Imagine the fullness of a day or week or lifetime in which you truly believe, with Julian of Norwich, that "All shall be well, and all shall be well, and all manner of things shall be well."[13]

As you return from your reveries, thank God for God's abiding love and eternal care for you and those you love. Trust that as you have imagined, your holy adventure will continue in joy, beauty, and justice.

On this last day of our adventure, you might choose to splash your images on paper with watercolors or colorfully draw them with crayons, with the invitation always to "color outside the lines."

LIVING ADVENTUROUSLY

You have come to the end of this book, but the holy adventure continues. What you imagined in the previous exercise can be lived out today and every day if you commit yourself to living God's holy adventure!

May your heart overflow with gratitude and praise as you celebrate over and over again the truth "This is the day that [God] has made; let us rejoice and be glad in it!" Be mindful throughout this day and in the days to come that not only are you on holy ground but also you can be the tipping point between life and death, joy and sorrow, wholeness and brokenness, everywhere you go.

Look for God everywhere, for indeed God is everywhere. God is "all in all!" Rejoice in your never-ending call forward in the holy adventure that is uniquely yours. Let the holy adventure continue!

Guide for Small Groups

Small-group spiritual formation and theological study are grounded in the interplay of commitment, appreciation, acceptance, and honesty. Persons need a safe and hospitable environment in which they can share their experiences and beliefs. The goal of small groups is mutual transformation in light of God's vision for our lives, not to win an argument or claim to have the right answers. As you share in forty-one days of adventure, surround your group and each member in prayer. Honor their uniqueness and special gifts. Listen to their deepest beliefs affirmatively. See Christ at work in each question and attempt to understand the challenges of faith and spiritual growth.

Diversity of experience and theological vision is healthy. When differences emerge, listen with care and affirmation, trying to understand what is being said in its best light. Remember that God is present in each person's life, even those with whom you disagree. One of the best ways to honor diversity is to see each person's vision as an affirmation and testimony. Accordingly, it is good to use "I" statements, such as: "I believe that God has a plan for everyone"; "I see God leaving many details of the future up to us"; "I am troubled by the idea of a God who plans everything"; or "'If God doesn't decide the future, how can I feel secure in this changing world?" If you find a member's viewpoint challenging, you may choose to reflect it back to him or her, perhaps by saying, "It sounds like you don't feel secure in a world where the future is undecided" or, "It sounds like you believe God gives us freedom."

The goal of small groups is to create and consecrate a holy space in which everyone can grow. Accordingly, generous times of silence and prayer may be helpful, especially if significant differences emerge. If your group has a designated leader, at such times, the leader might ask the group to take a few minutes to meditate or pray about the issue at hand.

I pray that your group will have a holy adventure in which God's lively adventure becomes the center of your lives and inspires you to become God's partners in healing the world. *Note:* You do not have to address all the questions in the guide; just use the ones you have time for.

INTRODUCTORY SESSION

(pages 7–22)

Spiritual Practice
- Time of silent prayer
- Introductions
- Sharing of one thing for which you are thankful today
- Prayer of thanksgiving
- Sharing of hopes for the group (see introductory paragraphs, pp. 205–206)
- Sharing of guidelines of respect, affirmation, and communication
- Read the story of Abraham and Sarah (Gen. 12:1-11).
- Reflect as a group on the most meaningful word or phrase in the passage.

Questions for Discussion
1. To what adventure is life calling you these days?
2. What spiritual practices or rituals do you regularly engage in? What are the challenges in maintaining a spiritual discipline?
3. What is your image of God? (Take time to draw a picture of God.)
4. Do you see God as a lawgiver? miracle worker? king?
5. What words do you use to describe God? What do these words tell you about God? What do they say about you?
6. Do you see God as personal or impersonal? In what ways is God personal? impersonal?
7. When have you experienced God's adventure in your life?

Closing
- Prayers of thanksgiving and intercession

Week 1

(pages 28–58)

Spiritual Practice
- Read Psalm 46, focusing on verse 10, "Be still, and know that I am God!"
- Silent meditation

Questions for Discussion
1. When did God become more than a word to you? When did God become real to you?
2. When have you felt God's presence most deeply in your life? What was it like?
3. What practice this week was most inspiring to you—affirmations, imaginative prayer, adventurous actions? Which one especially inspired you?
4. What affirmation during the week was most personally transforming?
5. As you reflect on your life, what new thing is God calling you toward?
6. When have you experienced divine synchronicity? How has it changed your life?
7. Do you consider yourself a cocreator with God? What difference does your life make to God and others? Do you think we can "surprise" God by our thoughts and actions?
8. Where are you most aware of the sin or imperfection in your life? in the lives of others? in the world? Where are you experiencing grace and love amid this imperfection?

Closing
- Pray, lifting up the imperfections and sins of the world and asking for God's healing presence.

Week 2

(pages 59–87)

Spiritual Practice
- Read Matthew 5:14-16.
- Meditate on the "light of God" (see Day 9).

Questions for Discussion

1. When do you feel most alive? What keeps you from feeling alive? In what ways can you claim more of God's lively energy?

2. How do you feel when you hear that you are created in God's image? Where do you sense God's image in yourself and others? What keeps you from experiencing God's image in your life? How would your life be different if you lived by this affirmation: "I am created in God's image"?

3. What do you consider your greatest gift? In what ways do you nurture this gift from God? In what ways do you hide this gift?

4. In what ways do you experience God's light in your life? What does it feel like? How often do you experience God's light in others? What happens when you remember to look for God's light in another?

5. As you seek to grow in wisdom and stature, what new ideas are you struggling with? What's too far out for you to venture? Where is God challenging you to launch out in deeper waters? How do you feel about God's challenge? (As a group or individually, draw a picture of the deep water and the treasures that lie below, awaiting your exploration.)

6. What are your greatest temptations as you explore your personal growth?

7. Where is your "quiet place" for prayer and reflection? How often do you take time for regular spiritual retreat?

Closing
- Share the areas where God is calling you to go deeper.
- Pray together for the courage to launch out into deeper waters.

WEEK 3
(pages 88–120)

Spiritual Practice
- Observe a time of silence.
- Read Matthew 25:31-46. Invite each person to choose a word or phrase that specifically speaks to his or her life situation today.

Questions for Discussion

1. Where do you experience God's blessing in your life? In what ways do you bless others?

2. Consider the "George Bailey Principle"—the significance of our smallest

actions in transforming the world. When have you experienced a small action making a tremendous difference in your life or in the life of another? What are the implications for our faith?

3. Reflect on the difference between living by abundance and living by scarcity. How do these different ways of living reflect our faith and trust in God? Do you live by abundance or scarcity? What about your faith community? What would it be like to believe that God will supply our deepest needs and that God's supply is inexhaustible?

4. How do you understand the interplay between giving and receiving? In what ways do you need "receivers" in order to experience your vocation? In what ways do you need to receive from others? Do you find it difficult to receive from others? If so, why do you think it's hard to accept the "kindness of strangers" and friends?

5. Reflect on the meaning of "doing something beautiful for God." How do you feel when you consider that your actions shape God's experience? How do you feel when you contemplate that your actions really make a difference to God as well as others? What would you like to give to God?

6. Take a look at your use of time and money. Do you hoard or share? In what ways does God call you to reach out to others, blessing them with your gifts of money and time?

Closing
- Consider this question: What beautiful thing can you do for God and for another this week?
- Count your blessings as a group, and thank God for the gift of life.

WEEK 4
(pages 121–47)

If possible, bring a photograph taken by the Hubble telescope or some other image of the cosmos in its grandeur. Bring a picture of something beautiful on planet Earth. Display these for the group.

Spiritual Practice
- Observe a time of silence; quietly listen for the "sighs too deep for words."
- Meditatively read Romans 8:18-27, reflecting as a group on where we experience the groans of creation. Have participants choose an image or phrase

that is spiritually powerful for them and share its importance in their spiritual adventure.

Questions for Discussion
1. Where do you experience beauty? What are your beauty spots?
2. Do you think the nonhuman world shares in God's aim at wholeness and salvation? How should we weigh our care for humans in relationship to our care for the nonhuman world?
3. In what ways are we called to live simply so that others—including the nonhuman world—can simply live?
4. How often do you take a "beauty break"? In what ways does the appreciation of beauty transform your daily life?
5. Read Psalm 8 meditatively. In what ways does this passage describe your experience of the universe? In what ways do you sense the grandeur of the universe? How do you think God cares for life beyond the earth?

Closing
• Conclude with a prayer of gratitude for the beauty and wonder of life in all its complexity and beauty.

Week 5

(pages 148–76)

Spiritual Practice
• A time of silence
• Read meditatively Mark 5:25-34, inviting each member to reflect on a meaningful word or phrase for a few minutes. Invite each member to share the word or phrase with the group.

Questions for Discussion
1. How do you define healing? Have you ever experienced or witnessed a healing? How does healing differ from curing? Is it possible to experience healing when a cure is not possible?
2. What social beliefs stand in the way of your appreciation of your body and the bodies of others?
3. What activities give you joy and pleasure?

4. What is your experience of complementary medical practices? How do these relate to your faith as a Christian?
5. Jesus often went to a "deserted place" to pray. Where is your personal "deserted place"?
6. In what areas do you need to experience personal healing? What practices promote healing and wholeness in your life?

Closing
- Provide an opportunity for healing prayer and anointing with oil. Persons may share their concerns or allow themselves to be blessed silently.

WEEK 6

(pages 177–204)

Spiritual Practice
- Time of silence
- Read meditatively Romans 8:37-39. What words or phrases seem most significant to you today?

Questions for Discussion
1. What is your vision of survival after death?
2. What do you fear most about dying? How does your faith shape your response to dying? Where have you experienced God's love being stronger than death?
3. Do you believe that persons receive rewards or punishments in the afterlife? Do our present lives make any difference in the nature of our afterlife?
4. What is your opinion about the doctrine of hell? How do you balance God's love and justice in your own life and in the lives of others?
5. What is the greatest insight you have received during this forty-one-day adventure? How has it changed your life?
6. What commitments to your spiritual growth do you intend to make in the future? What practices do you intend to continue in order to nurture your spiritual growth?

Closing
- A time of gratitude for the forty-one-day adventure
- A blessing of our future adventures ahead

Notes

PART ONE
Chapter 1

1. John M. Drescher, *If I Were Starting My Family Again* (Intercourse, PA: Good Books, 1994), 55.

Chapter 2

1. John A. Jungerman, *World in Process: Creativity and Interconnection in the New Physics* (Albany, NY: State University of New York Press, 2000), 40.

2. Ibid., 41.

PART TWO
Week 1

1. I use the number fifteen billion as a metaphor for the immense cosmic journey of which we are a part. Cosmologists have set the age of this universe from twelve to twenty billion years, and we can only speculate about other universes prior to or parallel to this universe. Still, I believe that we can affirm that God has always been creating, and that this creativity gives life to all things in their wondrous diversity.

2. Elizabeth Barrett Browning, "Aurora Leigh," in *The Oxford Book of English Mystical Verse*, eds. D. H. S. Nicholson and A. H. E. Lee (Oxford: Clarendon Press, 1917), lines 61–64.

3. I have been influenced by psychiatrist and spiritual guide Gerald May in my reflections on the interplay of noticing, pausing, and extending God's care. See Gerald G. May, *The Awakened Heart* (San Francisco: Harper San Francisco, 1993).

4. Mother Teresa, www.quotedb.com/quotes/2504; "32 Quotations from Mother Teresa," www.wright-house.com/religions/christianity/mother-teresa.html.

5. Martin Luther King Jr., *Strength to Love* (New York: Harper and Row Publishers, 1963), 107.

6. Frederick Buechner, *Now and Then: A Memoir of Vocation* (San Francisco: HarperCollins Publishers, 1991), 87.

7. Thich Nhat Hanh, *Peace Is Every Step: The Path of Mindfulness in Everyday Life*, ed. Arnold Kotler (New York: Bantam Books, 1992), 10.

8. Julia Cameron, *The Artist's Way: A Spiritual Path to Higher Creativity* (New York: G. P. Putnam's Sons, 1992).

9. Some texts read "master worker."

Week 2

1. Elie Wiesel, *The Gates of the Fores,* trans. Frances Frenaye (New York: Avon Books, 1966), 10.

2. To nurture your imagination, you might choose to meditate on James Weldon Johnson's poem "Creation" in *God's Trombones: Seven Negro Sermons in Verse* (New York: Penguin, 1990).

3. Robert Louis Stevenson, "The Lantern-bearers," in *Across the Plains,* quoted in *The Moral Philosophy of William James,* ed. John K. Roth (New York: Thomas Y. Crowell Company, 1969), 217–19.

4. Candace B. Pert, *Molecules of Emotion: The Science Behind Mind-Body Medicine* (New York: Scribner, 1999).

5. Julian of Norwich, *Showings,* trans. Edmund Colledge and James Walsh (New York: Paulist Press, 1978), 183.

Week 3

1. W. H. Auden, "For the Time Being," in *Collected Poems,* ed. Edward Mendelson (New York: Modern Library, 2007), 400.

2. For a more scholarly discussion of the woman who anointed Jesus, see Margaret Starbird, *The Woman with the Alabaster Jar: Mary Magdalen and the Holy Grail* (Rochester, VT: Bear & Company, 1993).

3. Alfred North Whitehead, *Process and Reality: An Essay in Cosmology,* corrected edition, ed. David Ray Griffin and Donald W. Sherburne (New York: Free Press, 1978), 244.

4. See M. Scott Peck, *People of the Lie: The Hope for Healing Human Evil* (New York: Touchstone, 1998).

5. For more on forgiveness and healing, see Kathleen Fischer, *Forgiving Your Family: A Journey to Healing* (Nashville: Upper Room Books, 2005); Flora Slosson Wuellner, *Forgiveness, the Passionate Journey: Nine Steps of Forgiving Through Jesus' Beatitudes* (Nashville: Upper Room Books, 2001); Tilda Norberg, *Gathered Together: Creating Personal Liturgies for Healing and Transformation* (Nashville: Upper Room Books, 2007); and Tilda Norberg and Robert D. Webber, *Stretch Out Your Hand: Exploring Healing Prayer* (Nashville: Upper Room Books, 1998).

6. For more on sabbath, see Tilden Edwards, *Sabbath Time* (Nashville: Upper Room Books, 2003); Abraham Joshua Heschel, *The Sabbath* (New York: Farrar, Straus & Giroux, 2005); Bruce G. Epperly and Lewis D. Solomon, *Mending the World: Spiritual Hope for Ourselves and Our Planet* (Minneapolis: Augsburg Books, 2004); and *Walking in the Light: A Jewish-Christian Vision of Healing and Wholeness* (St. Louis, MO: Chalice Press, 2005).

7. Bonaventure said this in his *Itenerarium Mentis in Deum;* this statement has also been attributed to a number of spiritual leaders, including Augustine of Hippo and Nicholas of Cusa.

Week 4

1. For more on Wisdom literature in scripture and other faith traditions, see Charles F. Melchert, *Wise Teaching: Biblical Wisdom and Educational Ministry* (New York: Continuum International Publishing Group, 1998) and Susan Cole, Marian Ronan, Hal Taussig, *Wisdom's Feast: Sophia in Study and Celebration* (Lanham, MD: Rowman & Littlefield Publishers, 1997).

2. Hildegard of Bingen, quoted in Matthew Fox, *Original Blessing: A Primer in Creation Spirituality Presented in Four Paths, Twenty-Six Themes, and Two Questions* (Santa Fe: Bear & Company, 1983), 57.

3. Robert Van de Weyer, comp. *Celtic Fire: An Anthology of Celtic Christian Literature* (London: Darton, Longman, and Todd, 1990), 80.

4. Patricia Adams Farmer, *Embracing a Beautiful God: Fifty-Two Stories and Lessons* (St. Louis, MO: Chalice Press, 2003).

5. "All Creatures of Our God and King," words by Francis of Assisi, 1225; trans. William H. Draper, 1925, altered. This text appears in *Chalice Hymnal* (St. Louis, MO: Chalice Press, 1995), no. 22. Used by permission.

6. For more information about Shalem Institute for Spiritual Formation, visit www.shalem.org.

Week 5

1. For more on the relationship of healing touch and Christian faith, see Bruce G. Epperly, *God's Touch: Faith, Wholeness, and the Healing Miracles of Jesus* (Louisville, KY: Westminster John Knox Press, 2001) and Bruce G. Epperly and Katherine Gould Epperly, *Reiki Healing Touch and the Way of Jesus* (Kelowna, BC: Northstone Publishing, 2005).

2. For a more detailed account of healing services, see Bruce G. Epperly, *Healing Worship: Purpose and Practice* (Cleveland, OH: Pilgrim Press/United Church Press, 2006).

3. Julie Dennison, "Not Less, but a Different Kind of Touch," *Christian Century* 108, no. 6 (February 21, 1991): 200–203.

4. For more on the relaxation response, see Herbert Benson, *Timeless Healing* (New York: Simon & Schuster, 1997).

5. This imaginative prayer is adapted from Bruce G. Epperly, *The Power of Affirmative Faith* (St. Louis, MO: Chalice Press, 2001).

6. For more on centering prayer, see M. Basil Pennington, *The Way Back Home: An Introduction to Centering Prayer* (New York: Paulist Press, 1989) and Bruce G. Epperly, *Spirituality and Health, Health and Spirituality: A New Journey of Spirit, Mind, and Body* (New London, CT: Twenty-Third Publications/Bayard, 1996).

7. Alan Jones, preface to Margaret Guenther, *Holy Listening: The Art of Spiritual Direction* (Cambridge, MA: Cowley, 1992), x.

8. Nelle Morton, *The Journey Is Home* (Boston: Beacon Press, 1985).

9. For a reflection on anger and lament in the Psalms, see Denise Dombkowski Hopkins, *Journey Through the Psalms*, rev. ed. (St. Louis, MO: Chalice Press, 2005). I am also indebted to my colleague Professor Julia O'Brien for her work on divine anger and justice in the Old Testament prophets.

10. Robert Davis, *My Journey into Alzheimer's Disease* (Wheaton, IL: Tyndale House Publishers, 1989), 59. I am grateful to Denise Dombkowski Hopkins for my initial encounter with this text in "Failing Brain, Faithful God," in *God Never Forgets: Faith, Hope, and Alzheimer's Disease,* ed. Donald K. McKim (Louisville, KY: Westminster John Knox Press, 1997), 21–37.

11. Davis, *My Journey into Alzheimer's Disease,* 107.

12. Ibid., 103.

13. Ibid., 110.

Week 6

1. "This Is My Father's World," words by Maltbie D. Babcock, altered, in *Chalice Hymnal* (St. Louis, MO: Chalice Press, 1995), no. 59. Used by permission.

2. Ibid.

3. Simone de Beauvoir, *A Very Easy Death,* trans. Patrick O'Brian (New York: Warner Books, 1965), 85.

4. C. S. Lewis, *A Grief Observed* (New York: Bantam Books, 1976), 69.

5. Ibid., 14.

6. Ibid., 55.

7. For other resources on bereavement, see Granger E. Westberg, *Good Grief* (Minneapolis: Augsburg Fortress Publishers, 2004); Bruce G. Epperly and Lewis D. Solomon, *Finding Angels in Boulders: An Interfaith Discussion on Dying and Death* (St. Louis, MO: Chalice Press, 2005); and Kenneth Mitchell and Herbert Anderson, *All Our Losses, All Our Griefs: Resources for Pastoral Care* (Philadelphia: Westminster Press, 1983).

8. For more on the distinction between "thou" and "it," mystery and objectification, see Martin Buber, *I and Thou* (New York: Simon & Schuster, 2000).

9. Created by Gerald G. May for the Shalem Institute, 1985. Permission granted by Shalem Institute, 5430 Grosvenor Lane, Bethesda, MD 20814 • www.shalem.org.

10. Mary Oliver, "The Summer Day," in *New and Selected Poems,* vol. 1 (Boston: Beacon Press, 1992), 94.

11. See Raymond A. Moody Jr., *Life after Life* (New York: Bantam Books, 1984); Karlis Osis and Erlendur Haraldssson, *At the Hour of Death: A New Look at Evidence for Life after Death* (Winter Park, FL: Hastings House Daytrips Publishers, 1997); and Kenneth Ring, *Life at Death: A Scientific Investigation of the Near-Death Experience* (New York: HarperCollins Publishers, 1982).

12. For more on universalism in Revelation, see Ronald L. Farmer, *Beyond the Impasse: The Promise of Process Hermeneutic* (Macon, GA: Mercer University Press, 1997), 163–93.

13. From *Revelations of Divine Love,* chapter 27, accessed at www.ccel.org/ccel/julian/revelations.txt.

About the Author

Bruce G. Epperly is the director of continuing education and professor of practical theology at Lancaster Theological Seminary. He is also copastor, with his wife, the Reverend Dr. Katherine Gould Epperly, of the Disciples United Community Church in Lancaster, Pennsylvania.

An ordained minister in the Christian Church (Disciples of Christ) and United Church of Christ, Dr. Epperly has written fifteen books, including *God's Touch: Faith, Wholeness, and the Healing Miracles of Jesus*; *Mending the World: Spiritual Hope for Ourselves and Our Planet*; *Walking in the Light: A Jewish-Christian Vision of Healing and Wholeness* (cowritten with Rabbi Lewis Solomon); and *The Power of Affirmative Faith: A Spirituality of Personal Transformation*, named by *Spirituality and Health* magazine as one of the best books in spirituality in 2001.

Dr. Epperly speaks regularly throughout North America on healing and wholeness, spiritual formation, Christianity and complementary medicine, process theology, ministerial wholeness, and progressive theology and spirituality. He has appeared on *Nightline, ABC World News Tonight*, and *PBS News Hour*.

He has been married to Rev. Dr. Katherine Gould Epperly since 1979, and they are the parents of a grown son, Matthew.

Beyond ministry and academics, Dr. Epperly's interests include walking, reading mysteries and spiritual autobiographies, travel, gardening, and cooking. Dr. Epperly is a Reiki teacher/master, spiritual guide, and spiritual coach for pastors interested in personal wellness and spiritual growth.

Other Titles of Interest

Forty Days to a Closer Walk with God
The Practice of Centering Prayer
by J. David Muyskens

Accept this invitation to an exciting and life-transforming journey through the gift of contemplative prayer. In forty days you will discover how you can be centered in prayer and centered in daily living.

The book teaches a method of prayer that goes deeper than verbal conversations with God. It teaches

- silent communion with God
- a method of being open to the gift of God's presence
- a way of receiving a deep and intimate relationship with God

Each day offers a scripture reading as a basis for the meditation that follows. J. David Muyskens includes stories from his personal experience and draws from a diverse collection of Protestant and Catholic practitioners of contemplative prayer.

ISBN 978-0-8358-9904-8 • Paperback • 140 pages

A thorough and friendly introduction to Centering Prayer (especially for lovers of scripture).
—Thomas Keating

To order, call 1-800-972-0433
or order online at www.UpperRoom.org/bookstore